SERVANT STUDIES
Resources for Servant Events

CONCORDIA PUBLISHING HOUSE • SAINT LOUIS

Published 2007 by Concordia Publishing House

Copyright © 2007 Youth Ministry Office
District and Congregational Services
The Lutheran Church—Missouri Synod

Copyright administered by Concordia Publishing House
3558 S. Jefferson Ave., St. Louis, MO 63118-3968
1-800-325-3040 • www.cph.org

All rights reserved. Unless specifically noted, no part of this publication may be reproduced, stored in a retrieval system, or transmitted, in any form or by any means, electronic, mechanical, photocopying, recording, or otherwise, without the prior written permission of the copyright holder.

The purchaser of this publication is allowed to reproduce the marked portions contained herein for classroom use. These resources may not be transferred or copied to another user.

Portions originally published by Youth Ministry Office of The Lutheran Church—Missouri Synod

Written by Steven Albers, Jim Gimbel, Donald Hinchey, Margaret Hinchey, Lisa Keyne, David Kruger, Tom Rogers, and Glenn Zander

Compiled by James Lohman

Edited by Mark Sengele

Unless otherwise indicated, Scripture quotations are taken from the HOLY BIBLE, NEW INTERNATIONAL VERSION®. NIV®. Copyright © 1973, 1978, 1984 by International Bible Society. Used by permission of Zondervan Publishing House. All rights reserved.

Scripture quotations marked ESV are from The Holy Bible, English Standard Version®. Copyright © 2001 by Crossway Bibles, a publishing ministry of Good News Publishers, Wheaton, Illinois. Used by permission. All rights reserved.

Catechism quotations are from *Luther's Small Catechism with Explanation*, copyright © 1986, 1991 Concordia Publishing House.

Your comments and suggestions concerning the material are appreciated. Please write to the Editor of Youth Materials, Concordia Publishing House, 3558 S. Jefferson Avenue, St. Louis, MO 63118-3968.

This publication may be available in braille, in large print, or on cassette tape for the visually impaired. Please allow 8 to 12 weeks for delivery. Write to Lutheran Blind Mission, 7550 Watson Rd., St. Louis, MO 63119-4409; call toll-free 1-888-215-2455; or visit the Web site: www.blindmission.org.

Manufactured in the United States of America

1 2 3 4 5 6 7 8 9 10   16 15 14 13 12 11 10 09 08 07

SERVANT STUDIES

TABLE OF CONTENTS

Introduction	7
1. Servant Event Devotions	8
2. Pre-Event Bible Studies	23
3. Multiday-Event Bible Studies	32
4. "The Way of the Servant" Studies	72
5. Worship Resources	90
6. Journaling	106

INTRODUCTION

For over twenty-five years, young people have been serving in the name of Christ through Lutheran Church—Missouri Synod Servant Events. The settings for this service have been many and varied: mountain camps and country churches, urban schools and inner city housing. The ser-vice has covered the gamut from building wheelchair ramps to creating camp trails, from roofing houses to hurricane cleanup.

Yet, beyond the different settings and tasks, one constant has been a part of these events: the opportunity to gather around the Word through Bible study, devotion, worship, and prayer. May this collection of *Servant Studies* provide young people the opportunity to serve in Christ's name as they gather around God's Word as His servants.

Our thanks to these dedicated LCMS servants who as Bible-study authors have given young people the opportunity to study God's Word at LCMS Servant Events:

Rev. Steve Albers	Leon Jameson	Rev. Dr. Joel Lehenbauer
Greg Arnett	Dr. Lisa Keyne	Rev. Dean Nadasdy
Rev. David Betzner	Rev. Mark Kiessling	Dr. Craig Oldenburg
Rev. John Brunner	Rev. David Koch	Rev. Tom Rogers
Rev. Dr. Jim Gimbel	Rev. Jim Kroonblawd	Rev. Dan Schumm
Dr. Don Hinchey	Rev. David Kruger	Rev. Glenn Zander
Margaret Hinchey	Bill Leese	Rev. James Zwernamann

Key to music resources used in Servant Studies:

LSB = Lutheran Service Book; LW = Lutheran Worship; HS98 = Hymnal Supplement 98; TLH = The Lutheran Hymnal; AGPS = All God's People Sing; SS = *Singing Saints*

SERVANT EVENT DEVOTIONS

The two devotional sequences that follow provide young people with a brief opportunity to reflect on and discuss their service. The devotions may be used individually prior to a one-day Servant Event. Use the entire sequence of devotions at the beginning or conclusion of the days of a longer time of serving.

I WANT TO BE LIKE YOU!

DEVOTION:
SERVING WITH ENCOURAGEMENT—LIKE BARNABAS

Opening

Distribute copies of the handout, divide group into two, and read responsively. Note that this same prayer handout will be used for this sequence of devotions.

We live our lives as servants in the name of the Father,
> *Who made us and keeps us alive.*

We live our lives as servants in the name of Jesus,
> *Who sacrificed His life for us and now lives for us.*

We live our lives as servants in the name of the Holy Spirit,
> *Who makes us grow in faith and obedience to be like Jesus.*

A Time to Memorize a Bible Verse

Christ died for us, Christ rose for us, Christ reigns in power for us, Christ prays for us! — Romans 8:34 (J. B. Phillips paraphrase)

A Situation for Reflection

Joel was a student at a Concordia University. He had started having a rough time meeting all of the expectations his instructors and friends had of him. Perhaps the hardest part was meeting his own expectations. One day when he was feeling quite depressed, he sought out one of the faculty members in order to share his anxieties and frustrations and to get some help and encouragement. The instructor listened well and gave some helpful words of encouragement, but something special happened a few weeks later. Joel found himself sitting next to the same instructor in a worship service where the worshipers were instructed to commune each other. When the instructor served the Lord's Supper to Joel, the instructor said, "Joel, this is what God thinks of you. Here is His Son's body and blood for you." For the rest of the service, Joel could only cry tears of joy.

- Tell of a time when you felt discouraged about something in your life.
- Who was an encourager for you? How did that person give you encouragement?
- How is the memory verse above a word of encouragement for you?
- How can you be an encourager to people you are with today—both fellow servants and those you are serving?

As you go through your day of serving the Lord, be an encourager to the people you serve and to those serving with you. Do it because God has told you what He thinks of you with His Son, Jesus Christ.

Can you repeat the memory verse? Say it as a group.

Closing

Sing "You Are My Own" (*AGPS* 270; *SS* 37). [Otherwise, have the males in your group read the first verse and refrain, the females read the second verse and refrain, and everyone read the third verse and refrain.]

Pray responsively in the same two groups as for the opening reading.

O Lord, we don't know exactly what will happen today,
> But we place ourselves and our lives in Your hands.

When we see opportunities to serve,
> Give us the encouragement we need to serve.

When we aren't sure of what we are doing,
> Give us the wisdom to ask for instructions.

When we are afraid of failure,
> Give us the courage to go ahead and try anyway, trusting in Your forgiveness.

When we are afraid of rejection,
> Remind us that you always love us more than anyone else.

Go and serve the Lord with His encouraging forgiveness.
> We want to be like You, Lord!

You may choose to collect the prayer handouts to use for next time.

Serving with Encouragement—Like Barnabas

Opening

We live our lives as servants in the name of the Father,
> Who made us and keeps us alive.

We live our lives as servants in the name of Jesus,
> Who sacrificed His life for us and now lives for us.

We live our lives as servants in the name of the Holy Spirit,
> Who makes us grow in faith and obedience to be like Jesus.

Closing

O Lord, we don't know exactly what will happen today,
> But we place ourselves and our lives in Your hands.

When we see opportunities to serve,
> Give us the encouragement we need to serve.

When we aren't sure of what we are doing,
> Give us the wisdom to ask for instructions.

When we are afraid of failure,
> Give us the courage to go ahead and try anyway, trusting in Your forgiveness.

When we are afraid of rejection,
> Remind us that You always love us more than anyone else.

Go and serve the Lord with His encouraging forgiveness.
> We want to be like You, Lord! Amen.

Servant Studies © 2007 Concordia Publishing House. Okay to copy.

Devotion: Serving with Joyful Witness—Like the Blind Man

Opening

Distribute copies of the prayer handout for this devotion sequence. Divide into two groups, and read responsively.

We live our lives as servants in the name of the Father,
Who made us and keeps us alive.
We live our lives as servants in the name of Jesus,
Who sacrificed His life for us and now lives for us.
We live our lives as servants in the name of the Holy Spirit,
Who makes us grow in faith and obedience to be like Jesus.

A Time to Memorize a Bible Verse

One thing I do know. I was blind but now I see! — John 9:25

A Situation for Reflection

Travis wasn't raised by Christian parents, but when someone told him about Jesus, that changed his life dramatically. All Travis could do now was live his life for the One who had died for him and now lives for him. One of the things Travis did was tell others about Jesus and what he knew about Him. Travis loved running in track and cross-country events, and, as a servant of the Lord, Travis even made his running an opportunity to tell others about Jesus. He would take along a portable tape player and some tapes with his favorite Christian songs to the track meets and play his music while he was going through his warm-up exercises. People would hear the music and words to the music, and, if anyone asked questions, Travis was more than ready to tell them what he could about Jesus.

- Do you know anybody like Travis?

- Would you like to be more like Travis? Why or why not?

- The memory verse above reminds us that we don't need to be experts about God or the Bible in order to share our Lord Jesus. Share what you consider to be the three most important things God has done for you.

Can you repeat the memory verse? Say it as a group.

Closing

Sing "Amazing Grace" (*LSB* 744; *LW* 509; *AGPS* 63; *SS* 2). Pray responsively in the same two groups as for the opening reading.

O Lord, we don't know exactly what will happen today,
but we place ourselves and our lives in Your hands.
When we see opportunities to serve,
give us the encouragement we need to serve.
When we aren't sure of what we are doing,
give us the wisdom to ask for instructions.

When we are afraid of failure,
> give us the courage to go ahead and try anyway, trusting in Your forgiveness.

When we are afraid of rejection,
> remind us that You always love us more than anyone else.

Go and serve the Lord, reflecting His love with your words and life.
> We want to be like You, Lord!

Collect the prayer handouts to use again next time.

Devotion: Serving with Joyful Perseverance—Like Habakkuk

Opening

Distribute copies of the prayer handout for this devotional sequence. Divide into two groups, and read responsively.

We live our lives as servants in the name of the Father,
> Who made us and keeps us alive.

We live our lives as servants in the name of Jesus,
> Who sacrificed His life for us and now lives for us.

We live our lives as servants in the name of the Holy Spirit,
> Who makes us grow in faith and obedience to be like Jesus.

A Time to Memorize a Bible Verse

And we know that in all things God works for the good of those who love Him, who have been called according to His purpose. — Romans 8:28

A Situation for Reflection

Jordan High School of Durham, North Carolina, had an awful losing streak in high school football. For four years they never won a game! That was a total of thirty-seven games!

How would you have felt if you had been a student at that high school?
  (Show your choice by a show of hands, and have two or three explain their answer.)
  angry   hopeless   depressed   hopeful   could care less/no different

How many football games would you have attended?
  (Show your choice by a show of hands.)
  none of them   a few home games   most or all of the home games

How do you think you would have felt as a member of that football team?
  (Show your choice by a show of hands.)
  angry   hopeless   depressed   hopeful   could care less/no different

The Jordan High School team finally did win a game . . . 36-14. In order to motivate the team, the coach not only gave the regular pep talk, he also said he would shave his head into a Mohawk when the team won a game. The motivation worked!

What motivation does today's memory verse give for playing the game of life even when things look hopeless? What is the ultimate good that is meant here?

As you go through your day of serving the Lord, remember the promise in today's Bible verse, especially when something hopeless happens. Remember that no matter what, you've been promised a place in heaven—the final victory guaranteed by Jesus.

Can you repeat the memory verse? Say it as a group.

Closing

Sing "Jesus in the Morning" using these verses:

Jesus, Jesus, Jesus in the morning, Jesus at the noontime,
Jesus, Jesus, Jesus when the sun goes down.

He's with me, He's with me, He's with me in the morning, He's with me at the noontime,
He's with me, He's with me, He's with me when the sun goes down.

Pray responsively in the same two groups as for the opening reading.

O Lord, we don't know exactly what will happen today,
> *But we place ourselves and our lives in Your hands.*

When we see opportunities to serve,
> *Give us the encouragement we need to serve.*

When we aren't sure of what we are doing,
> *Give us the wisdom to ask for instructions.*

When we are afraid of failure,
> *Give us the courage to go ahead and try anyway, trusting in Your forgiveness.*

When we are afraid of rejection,
> *Remind us that You always love us more than anyone else.*

Go and serve the Lord with the gift of God's loving presence.
> *We want to be like You, Lord!*

Collect the prayer handouts to reuse next time.

Devotion: Serving with Forgiveness—Like Hosea

Opening

Distribute copies of the prayer handout. Divide the group, and read responsively.

We live our lives as servants in the name of the Father,
> *Who made us and keeps us alive.*

We live our lives as servants in the name of Jesus,
> *Who sacrificed His life for us and now lives for us.*

We live our lives as servants in the name of the Holy Spirit,
> *Who makes us grow in faith and obedience to be like Jesus.*

A Time to Memorize a Bible Verse

But God demonstrates His own love for us in this: while we were still sinners, Christ died for us. — Romans 5:8

Devotion: Serving with Forgiveness—Like Hosea

Opening

   Distribute copies of the prayer handout. Divide the group, and read responsively.

We live our lives as servants in the name of the Father,
   Who made us and keeps us alive..
We live our lives as servants in the name of Jesus,
   Who sacrificed His life for us and now lives for us.
We live our lives as servants in the name of the Holy Spirit,
   Who makes us grow in faith and obedience to be like Jesus.

A Time to Memorize a Bible Verse

   But God demonstrates His own love for us in this: while we were still sinners, Christ died for us. — Romans 5:8

A Situation for Reflection

   Jim and Shelly had known each other since they were six years old. When they turned sixteen, their relationship turned into more than just a good friendship. They became boyfriend and girlfriend. But their relationship was not an easy one. Shelly had a difficult time being faithful to Jim. From time to time, she would deliberately ignore Jim and flirt with other guys—even being very promiscuous with them. One guy Shelly dated even beat her up when she didn't do what he wanted. After that incident, Shelly went back to Jim because she knew that he really cared about her. But then Shelly saw another guy who looked like more fun than Jim, and once again she ignored Jim. But no matter what Shelly did, Jim was always concerned for her and ready to take her back whenever she wanted him again.

- If you were Jim, how many times would you forgive Shelly? When would you stop taking her back?

- How is the relationship between Jim and Shelly like the relationship between the Lord and us?

- How many times has our Lord forgiven you for loving something or someone else more than Him?

   As you go through your day of serving the Lord, deliberately forgive and love those who aren't all that lovable because of who they are or what they do. Do it because that is what God the Father does with you.

   Can you repeat the memory verse? Say it as a group.

Closing

   Pray responsively in the same two groups as for the opening reading.

O Lord, we don't know exactly what will happen today,
   But we place ourselves and our lives in Your hands.
When we see opportunities to serve,

Give us the encouragement we need to serve.

When we aren't sure of what we are doing,

Give us the wisdom to ask for instructions.

When we are afraid of failure,

Give us the courage to go ahead and try anyway, trusting in Your forgiveness.

When we are afraid of rejection,

Remind us that You always love us more than anyone else.

Go and serve the Lord with the gift of God's loving presence.

We want to be like You, Lord!

Collect prayer handouts for reuse.

Devotion: Serving Despite the Risks—Like Rahab

Opening

Distribute copies of the prayer handout. Divide into two groups, and read responsively.

We live our lives as servants in the name of the Father,

Who made us and keeps us alive.

We live our lives as servants in the name of Jesus,

Who sacrificed His life for us and now lives for us.

We live our lives as servants in the name of the Holy Spirit,

Who makes us grow in faith and obedience to be like Jesus.

A Time to Memorize a Bible Verse

[Jesus said,] "I have come that they may have life, and have it to the full." — John 10:10

A Situation for Reflection

Mandy and Cath were spending an afternoon together at the mall. They had been having fun enjoying each other's company and looking at clothes. Mandy was startled when Cath said, "Hey! I like these!" and quickly stuffed a pair of earrings into a pocket. Mandy hadn't seen Cath do anything like that before. She wasn't sure what to say or to do.

- What risks does Mandy take if she confronts Cath?
- What risks does Mandy take if she reports Cath to a store clerk or some other adult?
- What risks does Mandy take if she stays quiet?
- What would you say and/or do if you were Mandy? Why?
- What example from the Bible can you use to explain why you'd do what you'd do?
- What risks are you willing to take for the Lord? (Show your choice by a show of hands.)

I'd die for the Lord.   I'd take some risks for the Lord.

I'd try to avoid the risks.   I would take risks if I was forced to.

I wouldn't take any risks.

🔨 The main message of the Bible is that Jesus came to rescue you and everyone else from sin and the consequences of sin. Look up John 1:10–12. When Jesus died on the cross, was there any guarantee that everyone would believe in Him and be saved? So what risk did He take when He died for you?

As you go through your day serving the Lord, think about risks you are taking in your relationships with the others around you—both fellow servants and those you are serving.

Can you repeat the memory verse? Say it as a group

Closing

Sing "Lord, I Lift Your Name on High" (SS 19). Pray responsively in the same two groups as for the opening reading.

O Lord, we don't know exactly what will happen today,
> *But we place ourselves and our lives in Your hands.*

When we see opportunities to serve,
> *Give us the encouragement we need to serve.*

When we aren't sure of what we are doing,
> *Give us the wisdom to ask for instructions.*

When we are afraid of failure,
> *Give us the courage to go ahead and try anyway, trusting in Your forgiveness.*

When we are afraid of rejection,
> *Remind us that You always love us more than anyone else.*

Go and serve the Lord with the gift of God's loving presence.
> *We want to be like You, Lord!*

Consider collecting the handouts to reuse next time.

Devotion: Serving Because of God's Love—Like Jesus

Opening

Distribute prayer handouts, divide into two groups, and read responsively.

We live our lives as servants in the name of the Father,
> *Who made us and keeps us alive.*

We live our lives as servants in the name of Jesus,
> *Who sacrificed His life for us and now lives for us.*

We live our lives as servants in the name of the Holy Spirit,
> *Who makes us grow in faith and obedience to be like Jesus.*

A Time to Memorize a Bible Verse

For even the Son of Man did not come to be served, but to serve, and to give His life as a ransom for many. — Mark 10:45

A Situation for Reflection

There were two youth groups from the same town who had a retreat together at a wilderness cabin that had the most basic of facilities. Among other things, the toilet had no plumbing. A "honey" bucket with liquid bathroom cleanser in it was under the toilet seat. In the forest, some 75 feet behind the cabin, was a covered refuse pit. When the bucket would start to get "ripe" or full, the custom was for the two presidents of the two youth groups to carry the bucket together and dump the contents into the pit.

What would you have done if you were the president of one of those youth groups?

🔨 I would have not attended the retreat so I wouldn't have to empty the bucket.

🔨 I would have attended the retreat but changed the custom so that everyone had to take a turn emptying the bucket.

🔨 I would have attended the retreat but changed the custom so that the adult counselors were the ones who emptied the bucket.

🔨 I would have attended the retreat and would have emptied the bucket even though I didn't feel like doing it.

🔨 I would have gladly emptied the bucket with the help of the other president.

Take a few minutes to explain why each of you voted the way you did.

Take three to four minutes to brainstorm on newsprint the most disgusting tasks you can think of. Then take a quick vote to determine which task is considered the most disgusting.

Let's say that in order to save the life of a friend you needed to do that most disgusting thing. How many of you would do it in order to save the life of your best friend? How would you feel if you were the best friend and your friend did the disgusting thing for you (show your choice by raising your hand): eternally grateful   thankful   relieved   surprised

According to 1 Corinthians 1:23, what disgusting thing did Jesus do for you? Remember that as you go through your day. Can you repeat the memory verse? Say it as a group.

Closing

Sing "Lord, I Lift Your Name on High" (SS 19). Pray responsively in the same two groups as for the opening reading.

O Lord, we don't know exactly what will happen today,
   But we place ourselves and our lives in Your hands.
When we see opportunities to serve,
   Give us the encouragement we need to serve.
When we aren't sure of what we are doing,
   Give us the wisdom to ask for instructions.
When we are afraid of failure,
   Give us the courage to go ahead and try anyway, trusting in Your forgiveness.
When we are afraid of rejection,
   Remind us that You always love us more than anyone else.
Go and serve the Lord with the gift of God's loving presence.
   We want to be like You, Lord!

THE IMAGE OF A SERVANT

Devotion: Christ for Me

Invocation

    Leader: In the name of the Father and of the + Son and of the Holy Spirit.
    Group: Amen.

Song

    "Father, I Adore You" (*AGPS* 94; *SS* 11)

Scripture Reading

    Romans 8:26, 28–39

Activity

    Divide into small groups. Each group should mime a life scene where someone might forget that God is with him or her. Others are to guess the scene.

Devotional Point

    Not only at this event, but in whatever we do and wherever we go, God in Christ is for us through faith, protecting, guiding, and saving us.

Discuss

    Why might we, at times, forget that God is for us? How does it feel to have this promise from Christ about our salvation and His presence in our lives?

Prayers and Lord's Prayer

Song

    "Make Me a Servant" (*AGPS* 174; *SS* 20) or "Open the Eyes of My Heart" (*SS* 24)

Benediction

    Leader: "May the God of peace, who through the blood of the eternal covenant brought back from the dead our Lord Jesus, that great Shepherd of the sheep, equip you with everything good for doing His will, and may He work in us what is pleasing to Him, through Jesus Christ, to whom be glory for ever and ever." (Hebrews 13:20–21)
    Group: Amen!
    Leader: Go in peace; serve the Lord.
    Group: Thanks be to God!

Devotion: Christ for Others

Invocation

    Leader: In the name of the Father and of the + Son and of the Holy Spirit.
    Group: Amen.

Song

    "Shine, Jesus, Shine" (*SS 28*)

Scripture Reading

    Matthew 5:14–16

Activity: Shadow Stories

    Divide into pairs; each person takes a turn using an overhead projector, powerful flashlight, or other light source to create a shadow picture of a Bible-story scene. Others guess what the scene is.

Devotional Point

    Shadows are difficult to interpret. If the light of Christ is hidden in us and doesn't come through, our witness to the message of salvation may not be clear. It is not our work to shine; Christ shines in us and through us.

Discuss

How and when might God's light shine through us on this trip? What can we do or say to make sure people see that the light is from Christ and not from us?

Prayers and Lord's Prayer

Song

    "Make Me a Servant" (*AGPS* 174; *SS* 20) or "Make Us One" (*SS* 21)

Benediction

    Leader: "May the God of peace, who through the blood of the eternal covenant brought back from the dead our Lord Jesus, that great Shepherd of the sheep, equip you with everything good for doing His will, and may He work in us what is pleasing to Him, through Jesus Christ, to whom be glory for ever and ever." (Hebrews 13:20–21)
    Group: Amen!
    Leader: Go in peace; serve the Lord.
    Group: Thanks be to God!

Devotion: Christ in the Scriptures

Invocation

    Leader: In the name of the Father and of the + Son and of the Holy Spirit.
    Group: Amen

Song

    "Lord, I Lift Your Name on High" (*SS* 19)

Scripture Reading

    John 8:31–36

Activity: Servant for a Day

    Divide the group into pairs. Have participants imagine that their partner is their personal servant for the day and tell each other what the day might be like having a servant. What tasks (appropriate!) would you have the servant do for you? (Things like homework, cleaning the room, going to athletic or music practice, chores around home, etc.) How does it feel to have a servant? How does it feel to be a servant?

Devotional Point

    Christ says that when we continue to read and study the Bible, we are His disciples and are set free. Some people believe that life in Christ is like slavery and not very exciting. Jesus assures us that sin is enslaving and that His Word in the Scriptures is light and life. We are free in Him.

Prayers and Lord's Prayer

Song

    "Make Me a Servant" (*AGPS* 174; *SS* 20) or "Holy, Holy, Holy!" (*LSB* 507; *LW* 168; *TLH* 246; *AGPS* 119; *SS* 15)

Benediction

    Leader: "May the God of peace, who through the blood of the eternal covenant brought back from the dead our Lord Jesus, that great Shepherd of the sheep, equip you with everything good for doing His will, and may He work in us what is pleasing to Him, through Jesus Christ, to whom be glory for ever and ever." (Hebrews 13:20–21)
    Group: Amen!
    Leader: Go in peace; serve the Lord.
    Group: Thanks be to God!

Devotion: Christ in Others

Invocation

    Leader: In the name of the Father and of the + Son and of the Holy Spirit.
    Group: Amen

Song

    "As the Deer" (*SS* 3)

Scripture Reading

    Ephesians 4:32–5:2

Activity: Servant Survivor

Form groups of six to eight. Imagine that the Servant Event is like a *Survivor* game. However, instead of voting people off the event, have each person, in turn, close his or her eyes while the rest of the group around the circle lists reasons why that person has earned the right to stay at the event.

Devotional Point

Servanthood is different from the rest of life. Even though we may be tempted to let servanthood become competitive, it isn't. We DON'T need to earn our right to stay alive on earth—or in God's good graces—by doing good works. God sees those deeds performed in faith and accepts them as praise for Jesus' sake. We joyfully serve because we are saved by the Master Servant. In Him, we are imitators of His love and care and forgive as we have been forgiven.

Prayers and Lord's Prayer

Song

    "Make Me a Servant" (*AGPS* 174; *SS* 20) or "Brothers and Sisters in Christ" (*AGPS* 78; *SS* 7)

Benediction

    Leader: "May the God of peace, who through the blood of the eternal covenant brought back from the dead our Lord Jesus, that great Shepherd of the sheep, equip you with everything good for doing His will, and may He work in us what is pleasing to Him, through Jesus Christ, to whom be glory for ever and ever." (Hebrews 13:20–21)
    Group: Amen!
    Leader: Go in peace; serve the Lord.
    Group: Thanks be to God!

Devotion: Christ for Servants

Invocation

    Leader: In the name of the Father and of the + Son and of the Holy Spirit.
    Group: Amen.

Song

    "To You, O Lord" (*SS* 33)

Scripture Reading

    2 Corinthians 12:9–10

Activity

    Identify a task that is impossible for one person to accomplish, like a smaller participant lifting the largest participant and carrying him or her from one side of the room to another or moving a rock or log that is too heavy. In front of the whole group, ask someone who cannot possibly do the task if he or she will do this favor and explain what the task is. When the person attempts the task, have the whole group offer words of encouragement. When that is not enough, select other volunteers to help accomplish the task.

Devotional Point

    There are many things we cannot do by ourselves. One is earning our salvation. Another is living a God-pleasing life. Yet another is being the perfect servant. Paul reminds us that when we are weak, God is our strength. Discuss how God has been our strength at different points during the week. Affirm that the greatest strength of God is His work for our salvation through Christ.

Prayers and Lord's Prayer

Song

    "Make Me a Servant" (*AGPS* 174; *SS* 20) or "Change My Heart, O God" (*SS* 9)

Benediction

    Leader: "May the God of peace, who through the blood of the eternal covenant brought back from the dead our Lord Jesus, that great Shepherd of the sheep, equip you with everything good for doing His will, and may He work in us what is pleasing to Him, through Jesus Christ, to whom be glory for ever and ever." (Hebrews 13:20–21)
    Group: Amen!
    Leader: Go in peace; serve the Lord.
    Group: Thanks be to God!

2

PRE-EVENT BIBLE STUDIES

Before departing on a longer Servant Event experience, you will want to bring together the youth for a time of orientation. These studies are designed to help young people prepare for their service and connect with the other young people who will be serving with them.

IMAGINE SERVANTHOOD

Warm Up: If I Were King or Queen of the Land

Break into groups of two or three. In each group, discuss and have someone record what each person would do if he or she were king or queen of the land. Then have each group create a top ten list of the best benefits and share the list with the large group.

Discuss: In our own daydreams, are we more likely to imagine ourselves in a position where we will be served or as servants of others? Why?

Opening Prayer

Lord, please be with us. Open our eyes to see that even as You came to serve, You desire us to serve others. Give us strength to do the difficult things in life, and fill us with compassion for all those in need. In Jesus' name. Amen.

Being of Service

Ask the group, "How do you feel about the opportunity to serve during this event?" Allow time for participants to respond.

Divide the group in half. Have one group list the blessings they have. Have the other group list things people around the world don't have but need in order to have a good life on earth. Compete to see which group can create the longest list in seven minutes. Compare lists to see if there are parallel patterns.

God Serves His People

Use a board or newsprint and markers to list ways God served the people in Bible times (Old and New Testaments). If desired, distribute copies of the reproducible Bible-study page.

What does Genesis 1:26–27 say about the character of Adam and Eve, the first humans God created? What is the image of God like?

What happened to ruin the image of God in people? (See Genesis 3:1–7 and Romans 5:12–14, 18a, 19a, 20a.)

Lest we think sin affects others but not us, read James 3:14–16. What does God's Word say about the presence of selfishness in all humans? What does James 4:1–5 suggest about how our natural selfish desires become evident to others?

Read Romans 5:6–11 and Romans 6:2–14. What significant event changed life for us?

The Greek word that is translated "servant" is the same word used to refer to "slaves." What does Romans 6:15–23 say about our former slavery to sin and our current servanthood in Christ? How are they different? How are they similar?

The true focus of faith is not on us—our failures as slaves to sin or our victories as God's servants. Christ is the focus of faith. What does Matthew 20:28 say about Him? How does His life model the image of servanthood for us?

God Uses Us

Create a list of ways God might use us as servants between now and when we leave for our Servant Event.

Have each participant complete this statement: "When I imagine servanthood in the light of Jesus Christ, these are its characteristics: …"

Closing Prayer

Dear God, thank You for reminding us that we are Your servants, able to live for You—though not perfectly—and fully forgiven and empowered by Your Holy Spirit. Open our eyes to the needs of others. Give us hearts that want to help and arms that will reach out to help others in Your name. Through Jesus we pray. Amen.

IMAGINE SERVANTHOOD

God Serves His People

What does **Genesis 1:26–27** say about the character of Adam and Eve, the first humans God created? What is the image of God like?

What happened to ruin the image of God in people? (See **Genesis 3:1–7** and **Romans 5:12–14, 18a, 19a, 20a**.)

Lest we think sin affects others but not us, read **James 3:14–16**. What does God's Word say about the presence of selfishness in all humans?

What does **James 4:1–5** suggest about how our natural selfish desires become evident to others?

Read **Romans 5:6–11** and **Romans 6:2–14**. What significant event changed life for us?

The Greek word that is translated "servant" is the same word used to refer to "slaves." What does **Romans 6:15–23** say about our former slavery to sin and our current servanthood in Christ? How are they different? How are they similar?

The true focus of faith is not on us—our failures as slaves to sin or our victories as God's servants. Christ is the focus of faith. What does **Matthew 20:28** say about Him? How does His life model the image of servanthood for us?

God Uses Us

Complete this statement: "When I imagine servanthood in the light of Jesus Christ, these are its characteristics: …"

Servant Studies © 2007 Concordia Publishing House. Okay to copy.

PRE-EVENT BIBLE STUDIES

I WANT TO BE LIKE YOU!

Opening

Each person should pair up with another person from the group. If there is an odd number in a group, have someone pair up with the session leader.

Have pairs face each other. The person whose birthday is closest to January 1 is to pretend that he or she is looking in a mirror. The other person is the mirror image or reflection. The person looking in the mirror should try to do the following actions, and the other person should mirror the actions as they are described by the leader (Have fun with this!):

- Make a smiley face (Be sure to be a good reflection!)

- Make a scary face

- Stick out your tongue

- Hop on your right foot and then the left

- Turn "right face," but turn your head to the left to look in the mirror

- Face the mirror again, but this time lean to your left as far as you can

- If the person looking in the mirror is a male, he should pretend to shave. If the person looking in the mirror is a female, she should pretend to put on mascara. The reflection should do whatever the other person is doing.

Now switch roles: the person who was the reflection now becomes the person looking in the mirror, and the other person becomes a reflection. Go through the same actions again.

Getting into the Subject

Distribute copies of the reproducible participant page. Whether we like it or not, we often end up being a lot like our parents. Even if we say, "When I grow up, I'll never [some characteristic of our parents we don't like]," we still end up being a lot like them. Individually, go through this list of characteristics and identify which parent you are most like as best as you can (circle the ones you choose):

height:	more like father	more like mother
weight:	more like father	more like mother
personality:	more like father	more like mother
hobbies/interests:	more like father	more like mother
facial appearance:	more like father	more like mother
taste in foods:	more like father	more like mother
taste in television programs:	more like father	more like mother

Pair up and go through the list again, but this time each person should give his or her opinion about the other person's resemblance to his or her parents. For example, "I think you have your mother's height instead of your father's." Are there more agreements than disagreements?

Getting into the Word

What Happened?

The apostle Paul was one of the great leaders of the first-century Church and the author of many of the books in the New Testament of the Bible. One of the things he strived to do was to lead by example. That's why he wrote, "Follow my example, as I follow the example of Christ" (1 Corinthians 11:1). Take thirty seconds to memorize that verse and its location in the Bible. Try saying it as a group.

In a sense, the apostle Paul was trying to be a mirror reflection of Jesus and encouraged others (including you and me) to be mirror reflections also. By seeing the things that Jesus, the apostle Paul, and others in the Bible did, we can learn how to be better servants of our Lord.

Taking a Closer Look

Look up each of these verses, and complete the sentence that explains the example given in each verse. Then grade yourself the way the Lord would grade you for that example.
(A = perfect, B = above average, C = average, D = below average, F = no resemblance at all)

Philippians 3:7–11
I have a hunger for _____ Jesus Christ.
   Your grade: A   B   C   D   F

1 Corinthians 9:19–22
I am willing to do almost anything for the sake of _____ someone else come to faith.
   Your grade: A   B   C   D   F

1 Corinthians 9:25–27
I train myself spiritually so that I practice _____-control.
   Your grade: A   B   C   D   F

Romans 1:9
I serve God with my _____ heart.
   Your grade: A   B   C   D   F

2 Corinthians 5:14
I am ruled and controlled by the _____ of Christ.
   Your grade: A   B   C   D   F

Colossians 1:3
I always give thanks for other Christians and _____ for them.
   Your grade: A   B   C   D   F

What Does This Mean for Us?

Look up and have someone read out loud Romans 3:10–12. According to these verses, what grade do we all deserve? Go back and change all of your grades above to what you deserve according to these verses. What's your reaction to this grade?

We aren't perfect, but we are forgiven. The apostle Paul knew that very well. What word of encouragement does he give in Romans 8:1? If there is "no condemnation," what grade does the Lord give us because of Jesus Christ? Go back and change all of your grades above to what God gives you because of Jesus Christ. What's your reaction to this grade?

Because of Jesus, we are forgiven and God sees us as perfect. But in our everyday lives, we know that we still have a lot of room for growing spiritually. What word of promise does the apostle Paul give in Philippians 1:6? What promise does he give in 1 Thessalonians 2:13b?

Each person should write out a prayer asking God to help him or her to grow during the Servant Event coming up. The prayer should include help in the specific areas identified as "weak" areas in the "Taking a Closer Look" section above. The prayer should also include thanks to God for the gift of forgiveness in Jesus Christ.

Closing

Go to the sanctuary of your church, and sit down in the chancel area, preferably on the floor behind the Communion rail if there is room, as a symbol of the fact that we can go with confidence to the throne of grace and receive the help we need (Hebrews 4:16). Ask for a volunteer to read Romans 12:1–2. Then each person can take a turn praying his or her prayer out loud as a way of committing to the Lord in response to God's mercy. Sing any favorite songs or praises that help you focus on God's love in Jesus Christ.

I WANT TO BE LIKE YOU!

Getting Into the Subject

Go through this list of characteristics and identify which parent you are most like as best as you can (circle the ones you choose):

height:	more like father	more like mother
weight:	more like father	more like mother
personality:	more like father	more like mother
hobbies/interests:	more like father	more like mother
facial appearance:	more like father	more like mother
taste in foods:	more like father	more like mother
taste in television programs:	more like father	more like mother

Getting into the Word

Taking a Closer Look

Look up each of these verses, and complete the sentence that explains the example given in each verse. Then grade yourself the way the Lord would grade you for that example.
(A = perfect, B = above average, C = average, D = below average, F = no resemblance at all)

Philippians 3:7–11

I have a hunger for _____ Jesus Christ.

    Your grade: A   B   C   D   F

1 Corinthians 9:19–22

I am willing to do almost anything for the sake of _____ someone else come to faith.

    Your grade: A   B   C   D   F

1 Corinthians 9:25–27

I train myself spiritually so that I practice _____-control.

    Your grade: A   B   C   D   F

Romans 1:9

I serve God with my _____ heart.

    Your grade: A   B   C   D   F

2 Corinthians 5:14

I am ruled and controlled by the _____ of Christ.

    Your grade: A   B   C   D   F

Colossians 1:3

I always give thanks for other Christians and _____ for them.

    Your grade: A   B   C   D   F

Servant Studies © 2007 Concordia Publishing House. Okay to copy.

3

MULTIDAY-EVENT BIBLE STUDIES

These studies for use during times of extended service—usually at least five days—give young people an opportunity to explore a Bible study theme and text. Through their study of God's Word and the power of the Holy Spirit, they can grow spiritually as they serve others with the love of Christ.

ARE YOU READY?

READY AND WAITING!

Leaders Notes

Are you ready? Readiness requires the ability to wait. There is preparation that occurs, and there is a willingness to go forward, but there is also the ability to wait for the right time, the appropriate signals, or for others to catch up with you and your plans or vision. Waiting is not the easy part of being ready. But, as Christians, we know that "waiting on the Lord" can be one of the critical factors in being ready.

Five of the bridesmaids were prepared for the bridegroom. They had thought ahead enough that they did not leave their lamps on during the night. The rich young ruler thought he was ready to follow Jesus, until Jesus told him to go sell all he had in order to follow Him.

We expect things so quickly and can receive them quickly in lots of areas in our lives. Being ready, though, requires patience, the ability to trust that God is at work in the situation. We may not see results quickly. An example at your Servant Event could be the new relationships you develop, but you may never know how your investment of time at this event impacts lives down the road.

Sharing—Hurry Up and Wait . . .

Ask the group to divide into groups of four by finding people they do not know as well yet. Distribute copies of the participant page. In their small group, have participants read the following and respond to the questions:

- Lucy met Joe at the junior prom. She thought they were having a lot of fun and was thrilled when he said he would call her sometime. That sometime still hasn't come.

- Mitch applied for a great job. The manager said she would call him within a week. That was eight weeks ago.

- Mandy cleaned out the basement while her parents were away for a week. Wow! She was covered with dust, spiderwebs, and dirt, but she got it done! She wanted it to be a surprise for her parents, so she didn't say anything. But they've been home almost eight hours and haven't said a thing!

Share something you have a hard time waiting for. What is your typical response when you have to wait for something?

Why is it so hard to wait? What makes it difficult?

Have you figured out anything that helps make waiting a little easier?

Read the Story

Read two stories: the parable of the ten virgins, Matthew 25:1–13, and the story of the rich young ruler, Luke 18:18–30.

What do these stories have in common?

Discuss the Story

What were the bridesmaids waiting for in Matthew 25?
How had they prepared for the groom's arrival?
Why were some of them unprepared when the bridegroom finally arrived?
What was the result of not being prepared?

What was it that the rich young ruler wanted of Jesus?
How had he prepared for what he wanted?
Why was he not prepared when he heard what Jesus asked of him?
What was the result of not being prepared?

Can you identify with anyone in these stories? The prepared bridesmaids? The unprepared bridesmaids? The rich young ruler? The apostles? Explain your choice.

Adapt the Story

Rewrite the story of the rich young ruler, this time providing a happy ending. What could have happened that would indicate he heard and understood what Jesus was trying to teach? Feel free to write a skit, design a picture, or change the imagery to help make the connection. Share your adaptations with the whole group.

Apply the Story

Return to your small group and share the answers to the following questions.

In which ways have you had to become a good "waiter" during this Servant Event?

Can you identify the values and the challenges of waiting? See if you can come up with three of each:

Waiting is good because . . .	Waiting is hard because . . .
1.	1.
2.	2.
3.	3.

Have participants re-form as a large group and collate their lists. Discuss with the whole group.

You are putting in a lot of work this week during this Servant Event. What are some of the things you have already accomplished?

You may never know the outcome of some of your work. What work or efforts might you make this week and yet never know the outcome?

What makes your efforts this week worthwhile?
What might those you are serving this week be waiting for?
How can you make the wait easier for them?

God's timing is something we do not understand and cannot identify on our calendars. "It is not for you to know the times or dates the Father has set by His own authority" (Acts 1:7). What might be one question you would ask God about His timing? After thinking about the question, read the following verse: "But I trust in You, O Lord; I say, 'You are my God. My times are in Your hands'" (Psalm 31:14–15).

As long as we are on this earth, we will have questions about why things happen, why other things don't happen sooner, and about our roles in making things happen. So many expressions remind us that waiting is not a bad thing. "Things take time." "Good things come to those who wait." But waiting becomes more difficult because so many other things have been sped up in our lives. Computers, cars, air travel, ATMs—so many tools can help us get more done, and get it done faster.

Waiting becomes a discipline, something that takes training and practice. But as Christians we realize the importance of waiting and letting God work in and through each situation. The phrase "wait on the Lord" is a reminder that God is active in our lives. "For my thoughts are not your thoughts" (Isaiah 55:8) is another reminder that we may not always understand the timing of situations. Hold on to the promise that "You are my God. My times are in your hands" (Psalm 31:15).

Prayer

Form a large circle. The leader starts the prayer and then others can share.

Lord, we have come to the end of another day of service. Thank You for providing for all our needs. We ask that You would provide restful sleep so we may be energized for tomorrow's tasks. We also commit to You those we are serving. We know they are waiting for _____, and we ask that You allow us to be your instrument in providing for their need. Teach us how to be ready for service and patient in our waiting. Amen.

READY AND WAITING

Sharing—Hurry Up and Wait . . .

In your small group, read the following and respond to the questions:

- Lucy met Joe at the junior prom. She thought they were having a lot of fun and was thrilled when he said he would call her sometime. That sometime still hasn't come.

- Mitch applied for a great job. The manager said she would call him within a week. That was eight weeks ago.

- Mandy cleaned out the basement while her parents were away for a week. Wow! She was covered with dust, spiderwebs, and dirt, but she got it done! She wanted it to be a surprise for her parents, so she didn't say anything. But they've been home almost eight hours and haven't said a thing!

Share something you have a hard time waiting for. What is your typical response when you have to wait for something?

Why is it so hard to wait? What makes it difficult?

Have you figured out anything that helps make waiting a little easier?

Read the Story

Read two stories: the parable of the ten virgins, **Matthew 25:1–13**, and the story of the rich young ruler, **Luke 18:18–30**.

What do these stories have in common?

Discuss the Story

What were the bridesmaids waiting for in **Matthew 25**?

How had they prepared for the groom's arrival?

Why were some of them unprepared when the bridegroom finally arrived?

What was the result of not being prepared?

What was it that the rich young ruler wanted of Jesus?

How had he prepared for what he wanted?

Why was he not prepared when he heard what Jesus asked of him?

What was the result of not being prepared?

Can you identify with anyone in these stories? The prepared bridesmaids? The unprepared bridesmaids? The rich young ruler? The apostles? Explain your choice.

Adapt the Story

Rewrite the story of the rich young ruler, this time providing a happy ending. What could have happened that would indicate he heard and understood what Jesus was trying to teach? Feel free to write a skit, design a picture, or change the imagery to help make the connection. Share your adaptations with the whole group.

Apply the Story

Return to your small group and share the answers to the following questions:

In which ways have you had to become a good "waiter" during this servant event?

Can you identify the values and the challenges of waiting? See if you can come up with three of each:

Waiting is good because . . .

1.
2.
3.

Waiting is hard because . . .

1.
2.
3.

Servant Studies © 2007 Concordia Publishing House. Okay to copy.

DON'T GET DISTRACTED!

Leaders Notes

Distractions get in the way of our readiness. It may be difficult to remain focused on the task at hand because of other things we allow to get in the way. Some of those things may look important, but are they really keeping us from the most important thing?

Ask each person to form a pair by choosing someone they worked with today. Then ask each pair to find another pair they didn't work with during the day to form a small group of four.

The first assignment is for each person to construct a list of personal distractions. Share some of your examples to get them started, such as watching television, getting a snack, and receiving phone calls or e-mail.

Each of those who said they wanted to follow Jesus allowed other things to get in the way. While those appear to be good and important activities, they were allowing them to distract them from what is most important—following Jesus and trusting all else would fall into place.

It has been said that "there is no such thing as an atheist." Everybody has something that is the most important thing in their life. In some ways that becomes his or her god. If I spend all my time and energy on hobbies, athletics, or work, that may keep me from remembering why I do what I do as a Christian. How do I stay focused?

There are times when we may miss an opportunity to serve if we are *too* focused and not open to the needs of the people around us. Jesus models how the interruptions from people were opportunities to share more about the kingdom of God. He always had time to answer questions, to heal, and to serve. But He also stayed focused on His task of sharing the message of salvation with as many as possible.

Sharing

Distribute copies of the participant page. Individually, have servants write a list of the things that are their worst distractions, the things that can keep them from accomplishing the task at hand or staying focused.

In your small group, share your lists, and construct one list of distractions. Do you have similar distractions? Identify the group's top three things/activities that cause the greatest or most common distraction.

Come together as a large group and list on newsprint the top three distractions from each group. Discuss what the distractions tell you about yourself and the group.

What are the most typical excuses for justifying the distraction?
What do your distractions tell you about your readiness for the task at hand?
Were there any distractions that almost kept you from coming on this Servant Event?

Read the Story

Today's lesson is not especially easy to understand. But it sure does help us think about what it means to be ready! In your small groups, read Luke 9:57–62.

Discuss the Story

Thousands of people were following Jesus. Some were truly interested in what He was saying. Some were wondering if He was indeed the promised Messiah they had been waiting on for centuries! Some wanted to see if Jesus really could perform miracles. And then there were those who were trying to trick Jesus to say something that could be proven to be false or that could be used against Him.

In this story, we have the example of several people who said that they wanted to follow Jesus. Can you imagine what Jesus' daily life was like? He traveled a lot, mostly by foot (and without Nikes!). He did not know where He would sleep at night or when He would eat next (and His disciples weren't good at meal planning either!). He had left His family behind and knew that one of His closest companions would betray Him. Not exactly what you would expect for a king!

- What excuses were used in these verses to demonstrate that each person was not quite ready to follow Jesus?

- What do their distractions tell you about what was important in their lives?

- What was Jesus trying to say with His responses?

- Do you think Jesus was saying that we should not take care of our families?

- "There is no such thing as an atheist. Each believes he is god." An atheist says there is no god. How does this saying fit the story?

Adapt the Story

Think about your service this week. A number of things may have distracted you from remaining focused on why you are here. In your small group, remind yourselves of the real reason you are here this week. What is your purpose? What is going to help your group remain focused throughout the rest of this week? Retell today's lesson, adapting it to your group and your Servant Event. Share your adaptations with the other groups.

Apply the Story

Return to your small groups and share the following:

- Do you remember why you came to this Servant Event? Share that with your group.

- What are some of the things that you had to give up in order to attend this Servant Event? Has it been difficult to do without those things this week? As a result of giving up those things, what have you accomplished?

- Yesterday, you discussed how waiting is difficult—particularly waiting to see the results of your work. How can waiting and the desire for acknowledgement be major distractions in a Servant Event?

- Some have said that time is one of the most important commodities in the twenty-first century. Everybody wants more of it—more vacation time, more family time, more time for volunteering, more time to learn and grow. What would you like to do if you had more time?

- Time, just like money, can be invested. Distractions can be seen as time wasters. How was your time this week an investment?

- How are interruptions by people different from distractions? Give an example. How did Jesus view the questions from people? Were they distractions?

- The theme for this week's Bible studies is "Are You Ready?" We may not always know the best process to get ready. But it can be very easy to identify what keeps us from getting ready. What are we getting ready for? What's the best way to keep our focus?

Prayer

Your group has made it through the middle of your Servant Event. Take seriously the comments about the distractions, and pray as a whole group that all may remain focused on why you are participating in this event and on the service you are providing. Commit the group's distractions to God, reading together 2 Corinthians 4:16–18 at the conclusion of the prayer.

> Therefore we do not lose heart. Though outwardly we are wasting away, yet inwardly we are being renewed day by day. For our light and momentary troubles are achieving for us an eternal glory that far outweighs them all. So we fix our eyes not on what is seen, but on what is unseen. For what is seen is temporary, but what is unseen is eternal. (2 Corinthians 4:16–18)

DON'T GET DISTRACTED!

Sharing

Write a list of the things that are your worst distractions, the things that can keep you from accomplishing the task at hand or staying focused.

In your small group, share your lists, and construct one list of distractions. Do you have similar distractions? Identify the group's top three things/activities that cause the greatest or most common distraction.

Read the Story

Today's lesson is not especially easy to understand. But it sure does help us think about what it means to be ready! In your small groups, read **Luke 9:57–62**.

Discuss the Story

What excuses were used in these verses to demonstrate that each person was not quite ready to follow Jesus?

What do their distractions tell you about what was important in their lives?

What was Jesus trying to say with His responses?

Do you think Jesus was saying that we should not take care of our families?

"There is no such thing as an atheist. Each believes he is god." An atheist says there is no god. How does this saying fit the story?

Apply the Story

Do you remember why you came to this Servant Event? Share that with your group.

What are some of the things that you had to give up in order to attend this Servant Event? Has it been difficult to do without those things this week? As a result of giving up those things, what have you accomplished?

Yesterday, you discussed how waiting is difficult—particularly waiting to see the results of your work. How can waiting and the desire for acknowledgement be major distractions in a Servant Event?

Some have said that time is one of the most important commodities in the twenty-first century. Everybody wants more of it—more vacation time, more family time, more time for volunteering, more time to learn and grow. What would you like to do if you had more time?

Time, just like money, can be invested. Distractions can be seen as time wasters. How was your time this week an investment?

How are interruptions by people different from distractions? Give an example. How did Jesus view the questions from people? Were they distractions?

The theme for this week's Bible studies is "Are You Ready?" We may not always know the best process to get ready. But it can be very easy to identify what keeps us from getting ready. What are we getting ready for? What's the best way to keep our focus?

Servant Studies © 2007 Concordia Publishing House. Okay to copy.

READY TO GO HOME

Leaders Notes

It does take energy to end a Servant Event and make the shift to heading back home with all the responsibilities, joys, and challenges involved. This Bible study provides personal, small-group and large-group time to think through the good that can be celebrated in the week, as well as one's personal readiness for heading home.

Ask participants to form groups of four that include people from different church groups if possible. Hopefully groups can form quickly and easily by now. Just watch to make sure all are included.

Here is real cause for celebration: "There is rejoicing in the presence of the angels of God over one sinner who repents" (Luke 15:10). Jesus loves us so much He wants all to repent and be saved. Are we ready to be at home with Jesus? Yes, we are ready as we believe in Him, knowing that because of His work—His death and resurrection—we have a place in heaven. Make sure servants understand "being ready" to be with Jesus forever is not based on good works but on His claiming us as His people.

Allow about eight minutes of personal time for servants to reflect on their own. Be available to those who may want to ask a question or share.

If your group is large, allow adequate time for all to walk around the room and celebrate the gifts of each other.

Sharing

Distribute copies of the participant page. In small groups, share the answers to the following questions.

- If you knew you were going to be stranded on a deserted island for three months, what is one item that you would want to make sure you took along with you?

- As you head home from this Servant Event, what is one thing you want to make sure you take home with you?

Read the Story

In small groups, read the parable of the lost son in Luke 15:11–32; then discuss the questions.

Discuss the Story

- Why did the son want his inheritance?

- The father could have refused his request. Why did the father provide the inheritance early?

- How did the son use his inheritance?

- When the money was gone, what were his options? What did he choose?

- "When he came to his senses..." (v. 17). It was not his first choice to go home. Why not? What was stopping him from going home to his dad?

- What was the father's response to his son's return? Why did it surprise the son?

- There's another participant in the story. What role does the older brother play?

- How does the father respond to the older son's complaints?

- If you were the older son, what would your reaction be after hearing your dad's reasons for the celebration?

- Read Luke 15:8–10. Why is the rejoicing part of this story so important? What is the ultimate reason for celebration?

Adapt the Story

You have worked hard together this week. There have been challenges, and there have been joys. In your small group, identify the reasons for rejoicing this week. Be prepared to share them with the other groups. You may want to pick one of your favorites and then try presenting it without words to the others. See if they can guess which incident you chose.

Apply the Story

Are you ready? Our week's theme helped us to think about being ready for our Servant Event. Were we ready to meet people from other churches and from the event site? Did we bring the right things? Were we committed to the task, or were we distracted by other things in the group or back home? Were we ready to *serve* and not be served? Were we ready to grow? Were we ready to share God's message of love and salvation in word and action?

- Now that you have come to the end of the week, share how you know that you *were* ready for this event?

- If you were to participate in another Servant Event, how would you prepare differently?

- Can you think of something that you wish you could have accomplished yet this week? What unfinished business might you be leaving behind?

Personal Time

On your own, think about the following: Are you ready to go home? Bringing things to a close can be difficult. You have new friends. You have been able to help those who may not otherwise receive assistance. You—hopefully—had fun and got to explore new places. Things back home may not be the most exciting.

- How did the lost son know that it was time to go home?

- What made it difficult to go home? What made it easy?

🔨 What was his reception when he got home? Did that make the effort necessary and worthwhile?

🔨 How are you like the lost son? What makes it difficult for you to go home? What is making it easier?

🔨 What else do you need to do to be ready to go home? Do you need to talk to someone, encourage someone, ask for forgiveness, or celebrate someone? Make a decision about what else you need or want to do before heading home. *Pray*, asking God to give you the strength for whatever needs to be done to help you be ready for your homecoming.

Group Time

Re-form your small group. If you would like, share any thoughts you may have from your personal time.

Your friends back home may not understand the joys and challenges you experienced this week. The older son in the story of the lost son had a hard time celebrating his brother's return, not understanding all the fuss. But the father had no trouble forgiving and forgetting what his younger son had done. He understood the homecoming was difficult for the son, and he wanted to *celebrate* the good—his son repented of his wrong, humbled himself, asked for forgiveness, and was willing to take a lowly place just to be with his father.

🔨 What is the ultimate homecoming for which we are preparing?

🔨 How do we prepare for our homecoming?

> But you, keep your head in all situations, endure hardship, do the work of an evangelist, discharge all the duties of your ministry.... I have fought the good fight, I have finished the race, I have kept the faith. Now there is in store for me the crown of righteousness, which the Lord, the righteous Judge, will award to me on that day—and not only to me, but also to all who have longed for His appearing. (2 Timothy 4:5, 7–8)

Prayer

Now that the week of working together is coming to a close, take a chance to celebrate the gifts of your teammates. Rejoice with each other!

Commit your leaving of this event and your homecomings to God. Pray for the person on your right and the joys and concerns he or she expressed about going home.

As Christians, we see each other as members of the Body of Christ. Our gifts complement each other. I may be a foot, you a hand, and our friend the nose. I understand that I have some gifts, and you have some gifts and that we are stronger as a result of working together towards the same purpose of worshiping and glorifying God in this world! Take time to go around the room and share with as many as possible "I rejoice in your gift of..."

Take time to celebrate the good things that occurred this week. Close the Bible study in large-group prayer. Commit the good events of the week to God, asking that He continue to work in and through the work that occurred. Put in His hands the actions and thoughts that need to be forgiven. Thank Him for His graciousness in providing opportunities for service. Ask for His guidance in helping all continue their service back home.

> We had to celebrate and be glad, because this brother of yours was dead and is alive again; he was lost and is found. (Luke 15:32)

> In the same way, I tell you, there is rejoicing in the presence of the angels of God over one sinner who repents. (Luke 15:10)

READY TO GO HOME

Sharing

In your small group, share the answers to the following questions.

If you knew you were going to be stranded on a deserted island for three months, what is one item that you would want to make sure you took along with you?

As you head home from this Servant Event, what is one thing you want to make sure you take home with you?

Read the Story

In your small group, read the parable of the lost son in **Luke 15:11–32**; then discuss the questions.

Discuss the Story

Why did the son want his inheritance?

The father could have refused his request. Why did the father provide the inheritance early?

How did the son use his inheritance?

When the money was gone, what were his options? What did he choose?

"When he came to his senses…" (v. 17). It was not his first choice to go home. Why not? What was stopping him from going home to his dad?

What was the father's response to his son's return? Why did it surprise the son?

There's another participant in the story. What role does the older brother play?

How does the father respond to the older son's complaints?

If you were the older son, what would your reaction be after hearing your dad's reasons for the celebration?

Read **Luke 15:8–10**. Why is the rejoicing part of this story so important? What is the ultimate reason for celebration?

Apply the Story

Now that you have come to the end of the week, share how you know that you *were* ready for this event?

If you were to participate in another Servant Event, how would you prepare differently?

Can you think of something that you wish you could have accomplished yet this week? What unfinished business might you be leaving behind?

Personal Time

How did the lost son know that it was time to go home?

What made it difficult to go home? What made it easy?

What was his reception when he got home? Did that make the effort necessary and worthwhile?

How are you like the lost son? What makes it difficult for you to go home? What is making it easier?

What else do you need to do to be ready to go home? Do you need to talk to someone, encourage someone, ask for forgiveness, or celebrate someone? Make a decision about what else you need or want to do before heading home. *Pray*, asking God to give you the strength for whatever needs to be done to help you be ready for your homecoming.

Group Time

What is the ultimate homecoming for which we are preparing?

How do we prepare for our homecoming?

Servant Studies © 2007 Concordia Publishing House. Scripture: NIV®. Okay to copy.

WHOPPERS FOR JESUS

THE SERVANT EXTREME: FISHES
LUKE 5:1-11

Objectives

- To discover what it means to follow Christ's call to be fishers of men
- To list principles describing the miraculous reality of the believer's relationship with Christ

Overview

Some calls request a response; others demand a response.

As a kid, Mom and Dad often called you by your name. Most of the time there was no particular urgency in their address: "Matt, are you about ready to go?" "Sara, don't forget your chores." "Chris, you have a phone message." Calls such as these leave the hearer with many options. We can respond immediately, delay indefinitely, or even ignore casually. There's nothing particularly powerful about such calls.

But then there were times when the tone and strength of the address changed. There was forcefulness behind it. If you were really in trouble, all three of your given names were used—loudly! Kids learn early that there are two calls, one of which means business.

In the same way, God calls to us all. One call can be seen through the Gospel message broadcast to the entire world. It announces God's grace and truth, His plan to save humanity and to judge sin. Those working and serving in the Church issue this call on God's behalf daily. It declares the options of life in Christ and life apart from Christ, and requests a response from all people through the Spirit.

Other times it is clear that God Himself powerfully changes the worldwide call into a clearly individual call to an individual believer. He drives His message deep into the heart of a particular listener, and through the Holy Spirit, the believer recognizes, without question, that God is calling his or her name.

Such a call is unmistakable. It demands a response.

Our Lutheran heritage equates this type of calling with the Holy Spirit working a faith response in our life, also called sanctification. It's what each of us experiences when we not only hear the Gospel message, but also are compelled to respond to its truth.

Have your students heard this call? Do they know the power of a compelling voice, challenging and demanding a response?

In your role as leader, you are a mouthpiece God uses to speak His truth to your youth. Youth need people of prayer and purpose to speak God's Word into their lives, not just stating the options and declaring the consequences, but urging them in the power of the Spirit to do something more with their lives than they alone ever imagined possible.

That's what this session is about: the miraculous, purposeful, eternally rewarding life of being a fisher of men. There's not a single believer who isn't called to this full-time, life-long vocation. If by the grace of God we've believed the call to salvation, we should by the leading of the Spirit respond to the call of evangelism.

Whoppers for Jesus: Leaders Study

"Come, follow Me, . . . and I will make you fishers of men" (Matthew 4:19). The entire game plan of Christian living and serving is found in this one concise statement: Follow and fish. The call Christ issued was so irresistible that the first disciples obeyed without knowing the first thing about what they were getting into—and that response was all right with Jesus. Their education in people fishing would follow as they learned from His lead.

At the start, the only obvious part was that the One calling the disciples had an uncommon authority, an authority in Word and action. From the reaction throughout the Gospel, it seems that unlike when most teachers of the day taught, people actually listened when Jesus spoke. And that catch of fish! Who could explain it except to say that God had done an amazing miracle through this man, Jesus.

Could Jesus bring a supernatural dimension to their lives? Could He lift them out of their work-a-day world and give them something worth investing their heart and soul? The disciples were convinced of it. They dropped everything to follow Jesus.

Consider what this text teaches us about entering into a miraculous life of fishing for people.

How to Get into the Fishing Business

1. Act in obedience.

Peter knew little about Jesus' life and identity at this point, but notice how he still called Him "Master" (v. 5) and "Lord" (v. 8). Peter recognized authority when he saw it. In the same way, Jesus does not expect us to become Bible scholars before we respond to the teachings of his Word and act in obedience to His command to "go" and reach others in His name.

2. Accept irrational assignments.

To an experienced fisherman like Peter, Jesus' command to "put out into deep water, and let down the nets" (v. 4) made no sense. Fishing in deep water in broad daylight just wouldn't work. But Peter obeyed anyway, just because Jesus said so. At the start, people fishing might seem hard and hopeless, perhaps even pointless to our human understanding. But no matter how irrational it seems, it does lead to miracles of faith, because Jesus is the one designing the assignment.

3. Admit your weakness.

After the miraculous catch, Peter fell before Jesus and pled his own sinfulness. Seeing God work in us, around us, and through us is a humbling experience. To remain humble and broken is essential, it is God who works in us, and we must not convince ourselves that somehow we are the ones in control.

4. Abandon your past.

The disciples left everything to follow Jesus. We can't hang on to our past lives if we want to be effective for the Lord. Leaving our "nets" is an important symbolic act in our walk with Christ. Undivided loyalty is required as we grow in prayer and ministry.

5. Anticipate overwhelming results.

In John 14, Jesus promised His disciples that they would do even greater works than He Himself did. Our "miracles" might not be as impressive as feeding more than five thousand people or making the lame walk, but they will be far more extensive. As the three thousand who came to faith on Pentecost demonstrate, when the Gospel is communicated by the Spirit's power, we, too, can catch boatloads of fish!

Whoppers for Jesus: Discussion Guide

Opening Experience

Ask—How many of you have heard of urban legends?

By definition, an urban legend is an often shocking story or anecdote that is based on hearsay and widely circulated as true (the urban legend of alligators living in the sewers); another name is urban myth.

Encourage the group to share example (s) of urban legends.

Say—The original urban legends used to mostly be about fishing! Many people consider fish stories to be whoppers—fabricated tales that are at least as much fiction as fact. What is the greatest fish story you've ever heard?

Activity Option

The Whopper—This is a unique activity for large or small groups. Instruct each person to tell the truth when giving two statements about himself, but to lie (tell a whopper) when giving a third. The whopper should sound reasonable and should not always be given last. Others try to guess which statement is the whopper.

Ask—When you hear fish stories (whoppers), do you usually believe them?

Bible Discovery

Say—God wants each of our lives to be a fish story, that is, a story of His amazing intervention in our everyday experience, a tale of miracles He works in the lives of people who believe in Him by faith. To demonstrate the real life whopper He intended for all people, Jesus worked a real fish story in Luke 5.

Read and discuss Luke 5:1–11

List a few similarities of fishing for fish and fishing for people.

- Peter was a professional fisherman. He was probably pretty decent at His job. What questions might have been going through his mind as he responded to Jesus' command in verse 5?

- Consider Peter's dramatic reaction to Jesus' miracle. What caused Peter to respond this way?

- Left on our own, success in this kind of fishing business might seem pretty daunting. What does Jesus' miracle say about our doubts about being a fisher of people?

- Through this miracle, what message did Jesus communicate about Himself and His mission?

What connections can we make between Jesus' command to be fishers of people and our work on this Servant Event?

Reflection

Jesus left everything to come to earth. Peter, James, and John left everything to follow Jesus. Jesus expects the same of His followers today. Share the variety of reactions people (like us!) often have to this command.

What do we need to leave behind in order to join Jesus in the "fishing business"?

What are some of the risks that such a "selling out" to Christ might involve?

How does the story from Luke help us face the risks of following Jesus?

Make a "fish list" of those in your circles of influence (your friends, family, people with whom you work) who do not know Christ. (Note: This activity can be completed in the personal journal of each youth, in a smaller group or with a partner, or through sharing with the entire group. Leaders should determine what approach best meets the needs and comfort level of their youth).

As a group, discuss the different ways the Holy Spirit can lead youth to "fish" for these people (prayer, inviting them to church or youth group, through serving, etc.).

Closing Prayer

Dear God, thank You for reminding us that we are Your fishermen servants, able to live for You—though not perfectly—and fully forgiven and empowered by Your Holy Spirit. Open our eyes to the needs of others. Give voices that proclaim You, hearts that want to help, and arms that reach out to help others in Your name. Through Jesus we pray. Amen.

THE UNTOUCHABLES

THE SERVANT EXTREME: HEALS
LUKE 5:12-16

Objectives

- To define sin and explain how leprosy illustrates sin's effects
- To recognize Christ's cleansing power and seek His touch for our sin sickness

Overview

It was on a trip to Boulder, Colorado, several years ago that I met an AIDS victim for the first time. Before then I had viewed the disease through the long, antiseptic lens of my television set. It wasn't really an epidemic to me. I didn't know anyone who had contracted the disease. While I understood the need for compassion, I couldn't seem to shake Romans 1:27 out of my mind when I thought about homosexuals with AIDS: "They received in themselves the due penalty for their perversion."

"Compassion is good," I thought, "but at the end of the day, lots of these people aren't innocent victims."

But the young man I met wasn't gay. He wasn't even an unbeliever. He was a Christian man who was newly married, had committed adultery against his wife once, and came away with the disease. I suppose I could say that he too reaped what he sowed, but in his case it seemed more like bad luck than "due penalty." His body was fading fast, but his heart was strong and alive. He was repentant and submissive to God.

I shook his hand.

Then I made a trip to the bathroom to scrub down. How many times had I been told that there was absolutely no threat from casual contact? Still, better safe than sorry. The truth be told, not only did I want to wash any trace of him from my hands, but earlier while we were talking, I was doing my best to avoid breathing his air. I wanted to love this man and be friendly toward him, but I hated his condition and wanted to be sure not to contract it myself.

"Love the sinner and hate the sin." That's the line we often hear about dealing with the muck of fallen human nature—and Scripture seems to reinforce the thought. Jude 22–23 reads, "Be merciful to those who doubt; snatch others from the fire and save them; to others show mercy, mixed with fear—hating even the clothing stained by corrupted flesh."

But "hating the sin" can't be used as an excuse for refusing others the personal touch and love they need to grow beyond their condition. That's what this story in Luke 5 teaches. There are times when ministers of grace must dive right into the mud bog of another person's experience. Jesus did it with the leper, with spectacular success.

Leprosy: A generic term applied to a variety of skin disorders from psoriasis to true leprosy. Its symptoms ranged from white patches on the skin to running sores to the loss of fingers and toes.

For the Hebrews, it was a dreaded malady that rendered its victims ceremonially unclean—that is, unfit to worship God (Leviticus 13:3). Anyone who came in contact with a leper was also considered unclean. Therefore, lepers were isolated from the rest of the community so that the members of the community could maintain their status as worshipers. Jesus did not consider this distinction between clean and unclean valid. A person's outward condition did not make one unclean; rather, that which proceeds from the heart determines one's standing before God (Mark 7:1–23; compare Acts 10:9–16). Therefore, Jesus did not hesitate about touching lepers (Mark 1:40–45) and even commanded His disciples to cleanse lepers (Matthew 10:8). Jesus even made a leper the hero of one of His parables (Luke 16:19–31).

The Untouchables: Leader's Study

As HIV-phobic as some people are, their fears probably don't compare to the attitude people in Jesus' day took towards victims of leprosy. In Bible times, lepers were completely cut off from the rest of society. They were forbidden to live in cities. They were bound by law to cry out "Unclean!" any time a healthy person approached. Worse yet, their condition was seen as a special judgment from God for their sins. Lepers weren't perceived as innocent sufferers, they were condemned as culpable criminals.

Given the hideous nature of the disease and its effects, the Bible actually does use leprosy as a type, or symbol, of sin. It is an apt physical illustration of the true spiritual condition in which we all find ourselves apart from Christ. This disease, which attacks the nervous system and renders a person without physical sensitivity, leads to all kinds of self-inflicted wounds—not to mention alienation from a frightened and repulsed society.

Thankfully, Jesus broached the cultural protocol, "risked" contact with the lepers of his day, and demonstrated with powerful miracles that grace could eradicate sin. Through healing miracles like the one we will study in Luke 5, Jesus waged violent war with Satan's kingdom. He announced the presence of the cure we all need most and at the same time modeled the kind of grace ministry that ought to characterize all of us who follow Him.

Just How Sin-Sick Are We?

1. Like leprosy, our sins cover us.

Sin is a disease that touches every part of our lives. Like leprosy, as sin progresses it renders our entire bodies insensitive to pain. Our sin is so all encompassing, and the Old Adam is so much with us, that we can't even recognize our desperate spiritual condition or make any kind of move to remedy it.

2. Like leprosy, our sins disfigure us.

Leprosy itself doesn't produce the kinds of grotesque deformities that are associated with the condition. Instead, because it desensitizes nerves, leprosy causes people to harm themselves, creating an ever-worsening set of injuries. In the same way, our sin when unchecked by grace does an increasing amount of harm to us.

3. Like leprosy, our sins blind us.

Some lepers go blind, not because the disease takes their eyesight, but because they never blink. As their eyes dry, their brains register no pain. In the same way, 2 Corinthians 4:4 describes our spiritual blindness: "The god of this age has blinded the minds of unbelievers, so that they cannot see the light of the gospel of the glory of Christ." We are blinded by a fog of our own making. Our sins obscure the truth of Christ so that we continue down our destructive path.

4. Like leprosy, our sins separate us.

Just as certainly as leprosy resulted in alienation from family and friends in Bible times, our sins cause radical rifts in our relationships. When lost to sin, we're kept from true intimacy and fellowship with others—and we're certainly separated from God in the most profound sense. This is the great tragedy of sin; it alienates us from the one person we were made to know intimately.

The Untouchables Discussion Guide

Opening Experience

AIDS vs. Acne. On chart paper or through discussion, list the obvious, and maybe not as obvious, differences between AIDS and acne.

AIDS	ACNE
kills many who get it	never fatal (despite feelings to the contrary)
no cure apart from a miracle	very treatable
don't see its effects immediately	highly visible
rare and frightening	extremely common
causes others to avoid those who have it	some sufferers even get dates

Bible Discovery

Given the chance to choose, do you think most people would compare their sinful ways to AIDS or acne? Explain your choice.

How is sin like disease, both for the victim and those around the victim?

Read and discuss Luke 5:12–15

- The man in this story did something illegal. Do you know what it was?

- He approached a healthy person and did not shout "unclean."

- Share your initial reaction to Jesus' response to the man.

- For what reason do you think Jesus told the man not to tell anyone about the healing?

- Jesus was probably sensitive to the hype surrounding His ministry. He wanted people to come to Him as true spiritual seekers, not thrill seekers. His time to be revealed had not yet come.

- Jesus said this man's cleansing was to be a testimony to the priests at the temple. At that time, before a leper was considered clean, he needed to show himself to the priests at the temple. What deeper testimony did this man have to share?

🗡 What does this miracle tell us about our sin? About God's attitude toward it?

🗡 In verse 13, Christ reaches out and touches the unclean man. What lessons about grace and mercy can we find in this miracle of Christ's touch that speak to our opportunities to touch lives through service this week?

Reflection

Leprosy deadens the sensitivity of nerves to pain, just as sin deadens the sensitivity of our hearts to the things of God. Because of Christ, we know renewed sensitivity to God in our lives. We see how our sinful ways grieve God's heart.

Sin grieves God. Thus, Satan would like for us to hide ourselves forever from the redeeming touch of Christ. How does the miracle in the story change our need to hide from God?

What unclean, "untouchable" issues in your life do you need to turn over to Christ?

Through His sacrifice on the cross, Jesus reaches out and touches all of us. The barrier of sin is no longer a disease separating us from Christ. When the man was healed, he went out and shared his news with everyone. How can you live out your forgiven life on this Servant Event? Back home? At school?

Closing Prayer

Dear God, thank You for washing our life of sin away through the blood of Your Son, Jesus Christ. Help us see that others around us are in need. Help us serve them in Your name so that others may see Your love, compassion, and care through us. Remind us that Christian service is not performed to earn us Your favor or blessing, but is done in thankfulness. Remind us that we were Your neighbor in need, and You sent Jesus to die for us and meet our need for salvation. In Jesus' name. Amen.

The Untouchables: Activity Options

Ashes to Ashes—This idea is not a new one but rather a recovery of a church worship practice that is easily used in a youth-group setting. This is inspired from a service for Ash Wednesday but is appropriate for use at other times of the year.

In a group setting, have the leader talk about sin and grace. (Make appropriate connection to Luke 5 and the servant event topic for the Bible study) After the talk, have students privately write down on a piece of paper a sin that is heavy on their heart, something that they want to ask God to be forgiven for (if participants are cautious about writing a word, encourage them to draw a symbol that represents the sin in their life). Collect the papers, and set them on fire over a nonflammable trash can, coffee can, or wok (have water or a fire extinguisher on hand for an emergency).

Collect the ashes, and after they have cooled, invite each student to place a finger in the ashes and turn to the person on his or her right and make the sign of the cross on that person's forehead. Adult leaders can also be identified to make the sign of the cross on the participants later that evening at a closing event for the day. This can be a powerful symbol to better understand sin, grace, and forgiveness.

Stone Reminder—Sometime prior to your Bible study, collect enough rocks so each person in your group receives one. Collecting these rocks may take some time, depending on the number that will be participating, but this is time well spent because each rock should, if possible, be quite different in shape, color, roughness, size, and other qualities.

The next step is to form a circle with your group. Ask the group to sit as close together as possible. (Around a campfire or bonfire would be a great setting) Before handing out the rocks, explain that each person will receive a rock and be given time to examine in great detail their own rock. Encourage them to pray that God would show them in their rock something that reflects their own life. (Example: the sharp edge on one side of the rock might represent sin in one's life that needs to be smoothed out and that like the water of a swift stream smoothes the stone, so God's Word working in us smoothes sin.) Have the group share what they chose with the larger group.

LET'S BLOW THE ROOF OFF!

THE SERVANT EXTREME: TEAM
LUKE 5:17-26

Objectives

- To explain the dynamics of teamwork in matters of faith and fellowship
- To evaluate and enhance the team spirit in our ministry

Overview

For years, United Airlines promoted its slogan, "Fly the friendly skies." It was a warm ad campaign, backed with piano accompaniment by Gershwin, intended to draw people into a kinder, gentler travel experience. But one particular commercial put a different spin on the theme. It ran something like this: "There's a place in the friendly skies that's not so friendly . . . it's the ten thousand mechanics of United Airlines . . . they're stubborn, picky, obnoxious . . . but if you fly, they're the best friends you'll ever have."

Nice thought. Brings some balance to the enterprise of air travel. "Hey, this isn't a carousel ride; it's a 500-mile-an-hour flight five miles off the ground! You'd better have some picky mechanics backing you up."

The same is true in the Church. There are times when we might like to think that being a Christian is all fun and fellowship, retreats and camps, wacky games and pizza. But there's an underlying seriousness to what we're about that calls for some gutsy people of faith to make sure our spiritual lives really fly.

In Luke 5, we run into a group of such people. They are no-nonsense, blue-collar guys who take Jesus seriously enough to send their friend on a flight right through the roof to meet Him!

It wasn't easy getting their paralyzed pal to the Lord. With a thick crowd of people blocking the way, it would be tough enough for one man to worm his way in, but these guys were dragging a stretcher. No way could they get through by conventional means.

But that didn't stop them. They hatched a plan to do a little friendly vandalism to the host's roof and airlift, or rather air-lower, their buddy to safety.

What safety he found! The original plan called for the paralytic to ask for healing. But before he could even ask, he found his sins forgiven instead. A physical healing soon followed. At the end of the day, through the hardworking faith of this dedicated team, Christ worked salvation. Maybe the sports cliché applies to the Church as well: "TEAM = Together Everyone Achieves More."

Let's Blow the Roof Off!: Leader's Study

When Jesus pronounced the paralytic's sins forgiven, the religious onlookers were scandalized. For different reasons, we may be too. It's not that we doubt Jesus' authority to forgive; it's that the one forgiven didn't say the magic words. He didn't say, "Jesus please forgive me; I repent of my sins." He just showed up and received salvation as a free gift.

When we put it in those terms, it doesn't sound so scandalous does it? Who of us didn't just "show up" and receive salvation too? This guy's story is our story. As a Lutheran, you recognize that faith is a free gift of God's grace. We don't even repent of our sins apart from God's prior work in our hearts to prompt repentance. In the case of the paralytic, Jesus did the work and took the man's very presence before Him as an expression of saving faith.

This brings us to a very important word in Luke 5:20: "their." When Jesus saw "their" faith, He called the man a friend and forgave his sins. What an extraordinary word! We almost always look at saving faith as a matter of individual response to the grace of God by the Spirit. But here is a collective faith that is just as potent. Some scholars have even suggested that it was the faith of the friends rather than the paralytic that brought about forgiveness and healing. Theologically that presents problems because no one gets saved on someone else's faith. But there's no denying that this miracle was a group effort.

Maybe the best application of this story is for students to recognize the power of faith exercised on behalf of others. When we intercede in prayer, we let our faith work for someone else. When we evangelize, we use our faith to point others to Christ. When we invite someone to church, we exercise our faith in a life-changing Lord to touch another's heart. In other words, we can be as undaunted as the team in this story and see how God works in the lives of those we encounter to make them forgiven and healed as a result.

How "Team" Works

1. A TEAM shows greater care.

It's always touching to see able-bodied people caring for those who are more physically challenged. The fact that these men even had a paralyzed friend speaks volumes about their care. They remind us of what was later written in Galatians 5:6: "The only thing that counts is faith expressing itself through love."

2. A TEAM promotes better cooperation.

Nothing of much value happens in this story unless these men work together. Getting a paralytic to Jesus in that day and age was a multi-man job. They did together what none of them could have done alone. If you've ever been part of a great team, you know the satisfaction of group success.

3. A TEAM fosters greater creativity.

It would have been fascinating to hear this team brainstorm when their way was blocked to Jesus. "Hey, let's tunnel in." "Nah, how 'bout we just yell fire!" "No, I've got it—we'll go through the roof!" High performing teams tap the potential of everyone's collective creativity.

4. A TEAM affords a higher cost.

We can't overlook the fact that to tear through someone's roof meant incurring an expense these men probably didn't anticipate paying. We don't know whether the homeowner held them liable or not or how expensive the repair was, but teams can pull together resources that many individuals cannot. Almost any important work ends up costing more than originally expected. Thank God for teams to foot the bill!

Let's Blow the Roof Off!: Discussion Guide

Opening Discovery

- Have you ever been a part of a great team—though not necessarily a winning team? What was most rewarding about your experience on that team?

- On this Servant Event, we are learning more about being part of a great team. What traits make our team most effective?

- What qualities do you think are essential to any successful team?

Bible Discovery

Scripture seems to indicate that the Christian life can be both an individual and a team activity. In what ways is your faith life individual? In what ways is it team?

Read and discuss Luke 5:17–26.

Setting the scene: List all of the different characters in this story.

(Jesus, the crowd, the Pharisees and teachers of the law, the paralytic and his friends)

As a group, use your imagination to retrace the steps of the paralytic and his friends from the time they decided to go to Jesus until they actually met Him. What obstacles had to be overcome?

Verse 20 reads, "When Jesus saw their faith . . . ." What is the significance of this phrase?

When you confess your sins, God hears and forgives you. What seems more impressive to you: to hear words of forgiveness or to see a lame man jump up and walk? What do Jesus' words suggest is really the greater miracle?

How did the man respond to Jesus' words of forgiveness?

What lesson can we learn from the man and his friends as we finish our time of serving this week?

Reflection

- How would someone define "team" when watching our youth group?

- How does teamwork express itself in our attempts to share the message of Jesus Christ?

- How is our teamwork being expressed in this Servant Event?

- What suggestions do you have for improving the teamwork we have been developing over the past few days in the following areas:

CARING   COOPERATION   CREATIVITY

From the story, it seems that good teamwork is found when Christians work together to bring not just physical or emotional healing to one another, but spiritual healing as well. How is our youth group a place where we learn more about faith and forgiveness through one another?

Closing Prayer

Dear Lord, thank You for loving us and granting us forgiveness for the times we fail You. Thank You for placing in our lives faith-filled men and women who encourage us in You and provide us with support and hope. Help us to serve You in what we do, think, and say. Help us to be caring, cooperative, and creative in our faith. But help us most of all to trust that we are Your beloved sons and daughters by Your grace through faith in Jesus Christ, our Savior, in whose name we pray. Amen.

Let's Blow the Roof Off!: Activity Option

Owl Island

The following simulation game is a great discussion starter for this Bible study rooted in team work, communication, and cooperation. It could also be tied in quite nicely with a devotion on the Church as the Body of Christ and the importance of each member. To introduce the game, explain that a mad scientist has cloned a deadly bacteria and that everyone in the world has been infected with it.

Divide the young people into groups representing the different countries of the world. Each country is to have theoretical biochemists, bionic men and women, and pharmacists. The theoretical biochemists are located in a top secret lab on the mysterious Owl Island. A vaccine effective against the bacteria has been synthesized at the Owl Island lab.

The task is for the theoretical biochemists to relate information about the vaccine via the bionic men and women back to the pharmacist in their respective countries. The pharmacist then reconstructs the vaccine using the information brought back by the bionics. The information they are sending is a description of the vaccine's structure (made of colored toothpicks and marshmallows).

The task must be completed within a given time limit. A country "dies" if the reconstructed vaccine is not exactly as the original or if the country is not finished before the time is up. The time limit can be made so that everyone or no one can have an opportunity to finish, depending on the leader's discretion.

Other rules:

1. Bionic men and women are used to transmit the information because Owl Island is surrounded by defenses such as booby traps, electrified fences, dangerous animals, and so forth. Therefore, only bionics can move between the island and their home country.

2. Only theoretical biochemists are allowed to view the structure, no one else. There should be some sort of screen set up so that no one else can see.

3. The pharmacists are supplied with toothpicks and marshmallows.

4. The bionics are not allowed to touch the toothpicks or the marshmallows. Only the pharmacists are allowed to touch them.

Suggestions:

1. It's best to have four to five people per group: one theoretical biochemist, two to three bionics, and one pharmacist.

2. The biochemists should relay the information a little bit at a time to relieve the confusion.

3. The distance that the bionics have to travel between the island and home country can be varied depending on how much you want to exercise the kids and how much territory you have available. It's great for camps.

4. The difficulty of the game is determined by the complexity of the vaccine. The more complex the vaccine, the more time should be allotted.

ROCK JESUS' FACE OFF

THE SERVANT EXTREME: SURPRISES
LUKE 7:1-10

Objectives

- To identify the defining features of a healthy faith
- To cultivate a greater faith in our lives

Overview

Main Entry: con·nois·seur

Pronunciation: kon-uh-sur, -soor

1: expert; especially: one who understands the details, technique, or principles of an art and is competent to act as a critical judge

A friend of mine is a baseball aficionado. He knows the obscure stats of players and teams the way most people know their own birth date. I can literally call out a year, and he can rattle off the starters of each team in the World Series. He is an avid collector of baseball cards and baseball merchandise. He plans his long-range schedule around the game dates of his favorite teams and players.

One of this guy's greatest memories is the day he bought a rookie card (of some baseball player I have never heard of) for a pack of Juicy Fruit gum from some kid off the street. He has a collection of eight or ten vintage cards that I think he'd save in a fire before his own family. Baseball is just his thing. He's a genuine baseball connoisseur.

Jesus is a connoisseur too. A connoisseur of faith. Nothing catches his attention or enthralls him more. In fact, only two times in all of Scripture do we see Jesus surprised or in a state of amazement. Once was in his hometown of Nazareth when those who had been closest to him refused to believe in him. Jesus was taken aback; the Bible even tells us He did not do many miracles there.

The second case of astonishment is found in the healing of the centurion's servant. Here was a man of completely pagan pedigree who suddenly shot past the entire nation of Israel on the faith scale. Jesus was astonished and declared, "I tell you, I have not found such great faith even in Israel" (v. 9).

Wouldn't it be great to be a person of such eye-popping, jaw-dropping, head-turning faith? the kind of person that makes others sit up and take notice? the kind of person that could even make Jesus take notice?

It's possible, you know. Through the Spirit in our lives, faith like the centurion's can become reality! The Bible tells us that God is waiting to take notice of people of faith.

> For the eyes of the LORD range throughout the earth to strengthen those whose hearts are fully committed to Him. 2 Chronicles 16:9

> I looked for a man among them who would build up the wall and stand before me in the gap on behalf of the land so I would not have to destroy it, but I found none. Ezekiel 22:30

This study is designed to identify what defines such a faith and what such faith can do in service to others.

Ultimately this is Jesus' faith. God counts His faith for our weak faith.

Rock Jesus' Face Off: Leaders Study

While the centurion's pagan background certainly wasn't helpful to him, his military background was. As a man under superiors, he knew authority when he saw it. Centurions were the backbone of the Roman army. They were like the gunnery sergeants or platoon leaders of today. They had just enough authority to be real leaders but were "grunts" enough to know how to respond to orders. Unlike so many rebellious, revolutionary people of Jesus' day, this man accepted his place in the pecking order and worked with the system. He even cooperated with the Jewish people he helped hold captive (Luke 7:4–5). On this particular day, his faithful spirit made all the difference.

Maybe that's why we recognize so few miracles today. We are not a people who respond well to authority. We tend to be overly individualistic and unimpressed by the power brokers in our world. We tend to not like working with authority, enjoy following, or accept submission, but the centurion did. His attitude, combined with God's Spirit, unlocked the miracle he desired and even the miracle of faith he did not expect.

Great Faith Means . . .

1. Great faith reflects Christ's character.

With just an initial reading of this text, we're struck by the Roman soldier's character. He cared for his servant deeply, despite the custom of treating them like property. (In fact, it was a social faux pas to express love or concern for servants.)

Second, he loved and respected the Jewish people and religion, as evidenced by his good relationship with the synagogue leaders. To see such mutual respect in such a hostile environment is amazing. The Jewish leaders even ran an errand for this man and pleaded his case! (Remember, the Jews were waiting for a Messiah to free them from guys like this centurion.)

Such "Christian" character was no merit in this man's account. It didn't earn him his miracle. But it does show that true faith has a transforming effect on one's heart.

2. Great faith respects Christ's righteousness.

Note how the Jews said, "This man deserves," yet the centurion himself said, "I do not deserve." He expressed true humility before the One whose righteousness far outshone his own.

3. Great faith recognizes Christ's authority.

This is the linchpin of the miracle. While most Jews required more and greater signs before they would trust Jesus' genuineness and benevolence, this man merely asked for the command. He knew the power of orders spoken by authoritative leaders, and he knew Jesus was just such a leader.

4. Great faith receives Christ's blessing.

Down through the years, we may wonder which meant more to the centurion: the fact that healing occurred or the fact that Jesus commended his faith?

5. Great faith releases Christ's power.

The bottom line: the miracle happened! The Lord did not do many miracles because of unbelief in Nazareth, but he did reveal His power for a believer, and culturally an outsider, like this man.

God calls for believers—large groups or single individuals—who will follow Him wholeheartedly, believe Him unquestioningly, and trust Him unswervingly. He even grants the power of His Spirit to make such faithful following possible.

Rock Jesus' Face Off: Discussion Guide

Opening Discovery

Looking at the world today, in what ways and in what places would you say that faith is expressed? (Think beyond the spiritual: Because of the advertisement, I have faith in the product that I purchase. I have faith in my hometown sports team to win the game, and so forth.)

Define the word *faith*.

(Hebrews 11:1 contains the classic definition, "Now faith is being sure of what we hope for and certain of what we do not see.")

Bible Discovery

Read Ephesians 2:8–9 and Romans 1:17. What do these passages tell us about the place and purpose of faith in our lives?

Read and discuss Luke 7:1–10.

Read the story at least two times. Describe the character of the centurion.

We know from the text that Jesus was amazed by the centurion's faith. What in particular do you think made his faith so outstanding?

Contrast the Jewish leaders' words in verse 4 with the centurion's words in verses 6–7. What differences do you see?

How might the difference between the words of the Jewish elders and the centurion's understanding of his position before Jesus help explain why so many people of the time did not understand the Messiah while so many Gentiles received him?

If you were to break this story into four or five key ingredients that define faith that is "amazing" to God, what would they be?

Reflection

Take some time alone to journal about your faith life right now. Where do you stand with Jesus?

Read Romans 10:17. What does it tell us about the source of our faith?

How has this Servant Event connected to your faith life?

Scripture is clear that we cannot earn our faith. Contrary to the words of the elders in the story, none of us deserves the healing of forgiveness—only Christ redeems us and makes us right with Him. Explain how your actions on this Servant Event are a response to the saving faith God has given to you—this is called living the sanctified life. What does it mean to you to live a life this way?

Closing Prayer

Lord, thank You for reminding us of the needs of our neighbor. Help us to reach out to others as we would reach out to serve You, but help us not serve for credit, acknowledgment, or any personal ego boost. May Your peace and spirit of righteousness be ours. In Jesus' name. Amen.

Rock Jesus' Face Off: Activity Options

Bag Affirmations

Give each participant a large paper lunch bag. Have each young person decorate a bag with his or her name. Set the bags out in your meeting space.

Encourage each person to write compliments and affirmations about others in their group. Leave the affirmation bags out for several days. At the end of your event, have youth pick up their bags and enjoy the encouragement from fellow brothers and sisters in Christ.

Affirmation Booklets

Assemble the following materials: colored paper, pens, pencils, markers, crayons, magazines, scissors, staplers and staples, glue, tape, and yarn. Then write the names of all the Servant Event participants (including the adults) on slips of paper. On the first day of the event, have each person draw a name to discover his or her secret friend for the week.

Using the materials assembled, each person makes an Affirmation Booklet, filling it with pictures, drawings, poems, Bible verses, and comments that will tell the secret friend what the person has learned about him or her. This can include what the person likes or admires about him or her, recognized talents, what he or she contributes to the group, what the person misses most about him or her when he or she is not around—anything that will affirm the secret friend. The goal is to keep this friend a secret by trying to get to know him or her without getting caught. The person must get to know several people in the process.

At the end of the Servant Event, gather everyone together for a prayer service, with time set aside to share the booklets. One at a time, each preparer presents the booklet to the secret friend, who reads it aloud. Then the recipient presents his or her booklet to his or her secret friend, and so on. Close the prayer service with a familiar song.

Affirmation Exchange

Want your group to know each other better? Give each person a sheet of paper and a pen or pencil. Have kids write their names at the top of the sheets. Underneath their names they should write, "One thing I really like about you is _____," and halfway down the sheet they should write, "A question I've always wanted to ask you is _____"

Now have them exchange papers, notice the name at the top of the sheet they have now, and finish each of the two sentences. Exchange several times so that each sheet has many affirmations of and questions about the sheet owner. When the sheets are returned to their owners, give the kids a few minutes to read what others wrote about them and to them. Then, one at a time, have your teenagers read and answer one question asked of them. Even if your group knows each other pretty well, there are bound to be some surprises.

FACING THE DEEP WATERS WITH A DEEPER FAITH

THE SERVANT EXTREME: TREADS
LUKE 8:22-25

Objectives

- To talk through circumstances and assumptions that cause doubt
- To draw lessons about living in faith from Christ's supremacy

Overview

Anyone can say they feel confident in the Lord during good times. Most believers would even say that they trust Him when life gets a little rough. But when all-out hurricanes strike, many people discover that it seems faith is gone with the wind.

You know the storms I'm talking about: The parent who promised to never leave walks out on the family. The school you had your heart set on sends you its final rejection letter. The grandparent you thought would always be there suddenly passes away. The seemingly perfect date decides you're less than perfect—good-bye love life.

It's in moments like these, and countless others, that we may be prone to groan.

"Where have You gone, God?"

"Don't You care?"

"Maybe You're not even there!"

Have you gone through such a storm of doubting?

I remember when my ministry meant moving my family from a place we had grown to love. I had always paid lip service to the idea of doing whatever God called me to do. I'd do what He wanted, anytime, anywhere. But when the call actually came, my family and I railed against God. I never knew how dependent I had grown on our city, our friends, and our safe routine. To have God call us to move away seemed impossible; He had to be kidding! But in reality, the only joke was the gap between my words and my actual commitment: Hey, God, I'll do whatever you want, anytime, anywhere . . . as long as it's here.

One of the greatest lessons the believer learns is that God allows storms. We recognize that faith grows in these kinds of conditions. Withholding such experiences would doom us to perpetual immaturity in our faith. Yes, it's true. God allows storms, but He is not the author of sin. Maturing in the faith means discerning between blaming God for the sin that causes storms, and recognizing His almighty hand in seeing us through the storms that come as part of a fallen world.

Despite our pains and doubts, we have a deep assurance that God's purposes will prevail. He doesn't test us to harm us. He tests us to strengthen us, and even as He allows the test, He also provides the solutions. Anyone who has come through a period of difficulty and seen the growth that results knows that perseverance is worth the effort.

Facing the Deep Waters with a Deeper Faith: Leader's Study

Luke 8:22–25 (and Mark 4:35–41) record an important nature miracle. This story has important theological overtones because of where it occurs, in deep waters. Throughout Scripture, the sea—or the deep—is an important theological symbol, serving as a metaphor for the world we live in now or the world to which unbelievers are headed. In other words, the sea or the deep is a symbol of destruction.

We see this symbol in the flood of Genesis 6. Noah builds an ark to save his family from the destructive waters of judgment. We see it in Jonah, where the sea rages as discipline against Jonah's disobedience. We see it in many psalms, where the writer cries out to God to not let him go down to destruction.

So against this backdrop, we recognize that Jesus is demonstrating His power over the forces of the deep, His supremacy over the doom we all dread. In this sense, this miracle is a parable of grace; all who place their faith in Jesus are saved from destruction. Thus the key question, "Where is your faith?" (Luke 8:25). God has merciful purposes for us, despite the destructive forces around us.

What Faith Refuses to Believe

1. Difficulties are never allowed by a loving God.

Many people are tempted to think that the devil or evil people or karma is getting the best of them when life goes south. But that is never the case with God's children. Everything is "father-filtered" in the life of a believer. So even though God is not the creator of our problems (that source is firmly found in our fallen nature), He still allows them for our long-term benefit. Don't buy the lie that difficulties don't come from His hand.

2. Difficulties show that God doesn't love us.

This is the classic fallacy concerning problems, the classic objection to the reality of evil: How could a good God allow this? Even the disciples fell into this one. When the waves beat against their boat, they cried out, "Teacher, don't You care if we drown?" (Mark 4:38). Of course He cares. There is no inconsistency between the presence of problems and the love of God.

3. Difficulties will wreck our lives.

Luke 8:24 records the disciples' cry this way: "Master, Master, we're going to drown!" That's all too typical. We think difficulty will result in utter destruction. "My life is over," we cry. But this is rarely God's plan. How often have your problems killed you?

4. Difficulties require desperate measures.

The disciples ran around in a fit of panic. Jesus slept. That's the perfect example for us to follow. As prone to action as we are, we need to remember that usually God simply wants us to rest in Him, be still and know that He is God, and trust in His deliverance.

5. Difficulties can thwart God's plan.

Not true. Look at the beginning and ending of the story, especially the way Mark puts it. The beginning: "[Jesus] said to them, 'Let us go across to the other side'" (Mark 4:35 ESV). The ending: "They came to the other side" (Mark 5:1 ESV). Sure there was a giant storm in the middle, but know this: if Jesus intends to take you to the other side, He will get you there!

Facing the Deep Waters with a Deeper Faith: Discussion Guide

Activity Option: Worst-Case Scenarios

Check out www.worstcasescenarios.com or the board game or book, and pull questions regarding disaster situations. Have four volunteers come to the front of the group, and ask each a question. If the volunteer gets it wrong (which he or she will because the questions are ridiculous), he or she must perform a physical, mental, or culture challenge. The volunteer gets to choose which kind of challenge to do.

Examples of physical challenges are shooting a spit wad through a straw using only one nostril, eating a hot pepper, or doing fifteen pushups. Mental challenges are things like reciting the Pledge of Allegiance, reciting the multiplication table for the number 8, or naming the capitals of certain states. Culture challenges are things like naming three of Shakespeare's plays, doing an interpretive dance to the Barney theme song, or improvising a made-up love poem to the guy sitting in the front row. As long as a contestant either answers a Worst-Case Scenario question right or completes a challenge, he or she stays in the game. If a contestant misses a question and cannot do a challenge, he or she is out. It makes it more interesting if each contestant is the representative for his or her grade and if the whole grade gets a prize if its representative wins.

Say—Sometimes when we go through storms in our lives we believe that they are a worst-case scenario. We may even find ourselves asking God, "Where have You gone?" . . . "Don't You care?" . . . "Maybe You're not even there!"

Opening Discovery

Share a time when you felt mad at God.

What are the greatest doubts you have in times like these?

What does our anger or doubt in difficult times reflect about our understanding of God? What is it we believe about life or about God that makes us respond this way?

Bible Discovery

Talk about the symbolic meaning of deep waters in Scripture. Almost every time we come across this image, it not only describes a physical condition, but also a spiritual reality.

Read and discuss Luke 8:22–25 and Mark 4:35–41.

What is the source of the disciples' fear in this story?

The disciples jump to the conclusion that they are going to drown. How is this a reasonable conclusion in one sense but irrational in another?

What does the fact that Jesus was sleeping teach us about Him? Why is this a significant detail to our understanding of the story?

What lessons about faith can be seen in this story?

Reflection

What is one big storm or difficulty you are facing right now?

Jesus asks His disciples, "Where is your faith?" As you weather storms in your life, where have you been placing your faith?

What kind of a faith response does this story call you to make?

How does a story like this change your perspective on facing the storms of life?

How can the faith lessons of this story connect to our experience serving this week? as we travel home?

Closing Prayer

Dear Jesus, thank You for being our wonderful Suffering Servant, giving of Yourself even to the point of death for our forgiveness and salvation. During the storms in our lives, help us to find strength in You. Strengthen us now for the storms ahead. Help us to remember that You are true to your promise that your purpose will prevail. Change us to be more like You in what we do and say, as we serve in Your name. Amen.

Facing the Deep Water with a Deeper Faith: Activity Options

Bucket Brigade

Supplies:

Cups, wading pools, 5-gallon buckets

Preparation:

Set the wading pools around the perimeter of the playing area. Set the buckets a few feet away from each other in the center of the playing area.

Form equal-size teams. Give each participant a cup, and instruct each team to line up single file behind a bucket. Each team's line should stretch in the general direction of one of the wading pools.

Explain that long ago, before cities had functioning fire hydrants and fancy fire engines, people used to fight fires by working together in bucket brigades. They would form a line near a lake or a stream and would pass bucketfuls of water from person to person all the way down the line until the water reached the burning building.

Tell teenagers that their job is to work together in their crew to move water from one of the wading pools into their bucket, using only their cups. They must do this bucket-brigade style, with the person at the end of the line pouring his or her water into the next person's cup, and so on. The last person in line should dump his or her cupful into the team's bucket in an effort to fill it to the top.

Once a team's bucket is full, it's time to put the bucket to use. However, instead of throwing water on a fire, they get to throw the water on one of the other fire fighting teams. The bucket carrier can get within 2 feet of another team to throw the water.

Once a bucket is empty, the team should begin working right away to fill it up again.

Rules:

1. Only the end people in each bucket-brigade line can move around, running back and forth to a wading pool, running to the bucket, or moving to douse another team.

2. The rest of the team must pick a spot and stay there. This means that players getting doused by another team cannot run away; they can duck or lean to the side to avoid being soaked.

3. Players are not allowed to sabotage the other teams' efforts to fill their buckets.

Other Group-Building Activities

Elephant, Kamikaze, Mosquito, Boppity Bop Bop Bop!

This fast-paced game will take some patient explaining and lots of practice runs to start out. The players should sit in a circle. Whoever is chosen to be "it" stands in the middle. "It" points to one person and says one of the following before slowly counting to five: "Elephant," "Kamikaze," "Mosquito," or "Boppity bop bop bop!"

When "it" says, "Elephant," the person pointed to should make an elephant's snout by holding his or her nose with his or her left hand and pushing his or her right arm through the crook of his or her left elbow. Meanwhile, the two people sitting on the sides of the elephant snout make elephant ears by touching their own heads with their outside hands. So the person sitting to the left of the middle person uses his or her left arm; the person on the right uses his or her right arm. All of this must be done before "it" has finished counting to five.

Give the players a couple of chances to practice this move, and then move on to demonstrate the kamikaze move. The person pointed to should form his or her fingers into circles and hold them up to his or her eyes—like a pair of glasses. The people beside the kamikaze make airplane wings with their outside arms.

Now add the mosquito. The middle person makes a V with his or her fingers and straddles his or her nose with it. Then the person takes the pointer finger from his or her other hand and sticks it through the V to resemble a mosquito's nose. The people on either side make the mosquito's wings by holding their outside hands up to their ears, with the thumbs pointed toward their heads.

Finally, add the boppity bop bop bop part. There are no hand motions for this one. When a leader points to someone in the circle and says, "Boppity bop bop bop!" the player pointed to must say, "Bop!" before "it" finishes saying the phrase. "It" is allowed to try to trick a player by saying only "Bop!" If the chosen player says "Bop" back, then he or she is automatically "it."

If any of the three people chosen to make an elephant, kamikaze, or mosquito mess up before "it" counts to five, then the middle player becomes "it," and the old "it" takes that person's place in the circle.

After the students get the hang of the game, "it" randomly chooses players to respond to one of the four calls. There is no set order for them. "It" should also be encouraged to gradually begin counting to five faster and faster each time to throw off the players. "It" can also add challenge to the game by calling different calls on each side of one person, who then has to use both arms to make different things.

4

"THE WAY OF THE SERVANT" STUDIES

The four readings that follow entitled "The Way of the Servant" comprise a study on the purpose of Christian servanting. The group could be gathered together in a secluded place either indoors or outdoors on four evenings for the oral reading of "The Way of the Servant" by several fluent readers. Discussion could follow, or each person could read his or her own copy of the discussion sheet silently and reflect on the content prior to a group discussion.

THE FIRST READING: GOD THE SERVANT

Picture if you will a high school graduation in some charming little Midwest town. It is one of those places where everyone is interrelated, where a yearbook is not needed because everybody knows each graduate and most of them will stick around for years to come anyway. Picture the night in the little auditorium in late May, when the humidity is hanging like a wool blanket and the "cool of the evening" is a joke.

Picture how, as each diploma is awarded to the twenty or so graduates, the parents step forward to accept it with their son or daughter, followed by an announcement of what that child will do after graduation: "Tom Barton, going to State University to study teaching. Judy Maurer, going to work for John Deere Quality Control. Russ Larsen is going into pre-ministerial studies. Matt Lawrence is going to be a servant. Kelly Haywood is off to . . ."

"A servant?" The whispers start; then a giggle or two erupts. Pretty soon the whole place is one great, repressed guffaw. "A servant!" That's what you do when you can't do much else. That's what you gotta do; nobody chooses to serve, let alone announce it at high school graduation. But then, you know Matt—always a little . . . er, different.

In fact, Matt isn't all that different. He's merely taking seriously what Jesus and almost two thousand years of followers have been saying: to be a Christian, one must be a servant—not figuratively or poetically, but lovingly. Still, the astonishment that would greet the high school audience is understandable. Our times place a low premium on this most exalted of offices—the office of servant.

To be servile is to be groveling, shuffling, and intentionally second class. Many would smirk in response to a suggestion of servanthood. The mark of success in these times, as indeed in all times, is not how well one serves but how many servants one can maintain.

Perhaps part of the problem with servants is that they are not a real part of middle-class American life. We encounter store clerks, waiters and waitresses, blue-collar and construction workers each day, but we hardly think of them as servants. If we were to refer to them as servants, they might be offended. Therein lies the problem: people take offense at being servants—as though it were dirty, demeaning, and degrading. We have difficulty remembering a time in American history when servants took pride in serving a master of importance. It takes a John Gielgud in the film *Arthur* to remind us that the servant performs a unique task for the master—that of loving care. Gielgud's character would fume and fret like a mother hen with the "master" who was acting in a less than gentlemanly way, and he would use whatever authority he had (which was considerable) in order to restore the master to his proper place. This from a servant, mind you.

So, two problems arise. First, we handle servanthood very badly as a society. Second, the servants in our society don't quite know how to wear the servant's uniform with much class.

But there is a deeper problem: the assumption (sometimes not too well hidden) that "getting ahead" is measured by how much money we earn or how many people we push around (formally stated: wealth and power).

I once asked a very bright high school graduate what his career plans were. "Medicine," he answered, "I want to be a doctor." After I extolled his humanitarian concern for a minute or two, he explained, "No, it's not for any of that service-to-mankind stuff. I want to make enough money to retire by forty. Then I can have some real fun!" What worried me was that he said that without blushing, and what saddened me was that he really believed it. If the goal of an eighteen-year-old's life is having "some real fun," then there must be some weeping for a life wasted. Certainly God means more for us—and what He means is servanthood.

Why Serve?

If we were to do a verse by verse study of "servant" passages in the Bible, we would first be impressed by the sheer number of references. There are over 1,300 references to *servant*, *service*, and *serve* in one concordance of the Revised Standard Version of the Bible! Our second impression would be feeling the obligation to serve. "If anyone wants to be first, he must be the very last, and the servant of all," Jesus tells His disciples (Mark 9:35). After our Lord washes the disciples' feet (John 13), He commands His disciples that because they are not above their Master, they also should be in the servant role to one another. You can't read successively many chapters in any Gospel of the New Testament without running into Jesus commanding service. So, if asked, "Why be a servant?" the very simple answer would be, "Because Jesus told me to." There's nothing really wrong with that. After all, Jesus is Lord; I'm not. I'd best do what He says.

However, doing something because someone else says we should is a pretty sour motivation. If you don't believe that, think of that last time you mowed the lawn because your dad told you to. There was not a leaping joy in your heart as you made the rounds! In theological jargon, that's called "living by the Law," and while it gets the job done, it does not strike the heart of the servant at a level of profound discipleship. You can only get so much mileage out of Law-living; then you begin to turn irritated, angry, and resentful. Jesus told a number of parables about folk who were Law-livers, not true servants: the elder brother in the parable of the prodigal son, the laborers who were paid the same as those hired later, the rich young ruler who wanted to know what to do in order to be saved. All of these were serving because they felt the compulsion to serve. All went away empty-handed because God's idea of service is something far more deeply rooted in His purposes for us than a mere following of a command. Indeed, Jesus does give His disciples a command to serve and if, in a given situation, you can't think of one good earthly reason to serve, that command might have to do for the time being as motivation. But there is a better reason.

Service Is Love Enacted

My serving you is a dramatization of my love for you. I you are a Christian, that is, one who is baptized into the death and resurrection of Christ Jesus, then you realize that talk is cheap. Ours is a God who will never stop at saying, "I love you"; He does love. From His first recorded deed of love (see Genesis 1–2 accounts of creation) to Jesus' last recorded love words to Peter (see John 21), the legacy of all Scripture is that service in the name of Jesus is carrying on the love of the Father and of the Son. If, in fact, the meaning of life is the sharing of love—and Christian people would confess that a "good life" is a life lived in love of God and of His people—then service is the vehicle by which that love is shared.

The First Article: God the Servant

"Why did God create the world?" Kids have a way of asking those questions of parents on the way home from church (which probably explains why some parents don't like to come to church). But it's a good question. It's also a pretty open question because the Genesis accounts don't tell us the "why" of creation (nor the "how"—something to remember in all those debates about creation versus evolution).

Theologians over the years have speculated that given God's endless capacity for loving, He created out of love. He was not bored, nor did He itch to do something exciting. That powerful yearning to love within the breast of God needed an object, and so God created so that He can love. God's love toward us results in an act of service—His creating.

I recall once reading a Bible study in which the author pointed out that workers should feel particularly at home in the Christian religion because their God is a Workman (albeit with a capital "W" on Workman). The first image of God that comes to us in the Bible is that of God as a Craftsman—a Workman! He stretches a firmament and gathers the waters. He's the Divine Farmer as the earth brings forth vegetation. He fashions the lights for the heavens and in a marvelous way creates the monsters of the sea, birds of the air, and animals for the land. Then, as the final crowning touch of all creation, He gently forms Adam, the man, from mud of the ground, a clay-splattered Sculptor in some long ago tropical studio. Isaiah later picks up on that picture when he sarcastically wonders how the pot will ever dare to question the potter's creating (Isaiah 45:9).

My initial reaction to this observation was offense. How dare this theologian put God the Lord on the same level as some working servant? But that says more about me and my values than it does about the theologian. Who says that working, fashioning, sculpting, and serving are antithetical to God's lordliness? Why do I assume that God's loving act of creation is not a serving act? Might it not become impulse on my part to be Lord rather than servant? Perhaps lordliness and servanthood are all wrapped up in the same package. They certainly were for God on the first day of creation. He exercises lordship by serving creation.

Luther's explanation of the First Article of the Creed takes a passing swing at the idea when he concludes: "All this (His creation and preservation) He does only out of fatherly, divine goodness and mercy . . . For all this it is my duty to thank and praise, serve and obey Him." Because God in His inexhaustible love creates and preserves—becomes the servant for me—it is my duty to serve Him. But God acts first.

I serve Him not only because I have to (and I do have to) or because I am commanded to (and I am commanded to) but also because I am loved into it. My world is born out of God's love, and His continuing creation stretches through the years from this same root of love. My own personal history begins in the love of parents for one another, and I enter the world by being served. Service is such a natural and graceful part of my existence that when I read Jesus' words, "If anyone wants to be first, he must be the very last, and the servant of all," they ring true because He says it and because His disciples know that servanthood is the natural way of loving.

THE WAY OF THE SERVANT

DISCUSSION QUESTIONS ON THE FIRST READING

1. Tell about a servant who has served you recently (today?). How did he or she serve you? With what attitude or spirit? How did you react to his or her service?

2. Describe in your own words what "living by the law" means to you. Can you remember an incident in your own life when you served because someone told you to? What were your feelings? How did your feelings affect your service?

3. Think of some recent television programs or commercials that promote the idea that "getting ahead" is measurable in terms of how much money we earn or how many people we push around. How do you react to such a message?

4. How do you feel about the image of God as a blue-collar workman? How does that image impact your feelings about God?

Servant Studies © 2007 Concordia Publishing House. Okay to copy.

THE SECOND READING: CHRIST THE SERVANT

> He (Jesus) healed all their sick, warning them not to tell who He was. This was to fulfill what was spoken through His prophet Isaiah: "Here is My servant whom I have chosen, the one I love, in whom I delight." (Matthew 12:15–21)

Our last reading focused on God as the servant. Because He loves, He serves and He calls on His creation to join with Him in serving. The Second Article of the Apostles' Creed—the article dealing with Jesus the Christ—presents to us God's servant par excellence. "Like father, like son," so the saying goes, and it's particularly true here. Jesus' mission was to save—that's true—but His saving came through serving. Unlike the medieval knights with shining armor and brandished sword, Jesus does battle with the dragon of death by submitting to it. He has no Merlin-like formula for eradicating sin, save the service of the sin-scarred. Part of the passage above is a quote from Isaiah (42:1–4), which Matthew cites in order to show that Jesus is Isaiah's prophesied "servant."

In the latter chapters of Isaiah, we are introduced to the chosen man of God, bathed in God's Spirit. He is a quiet bringer of justice to the nations (all nations, not only Israel) and a gentle, dauntless messenger of God in a time of lawlessness and chaos. Some scholars see a reference to the whole nation of Israel in this poem; others see a reference to a specific individual. The Church of Jesus Christ, however, sees a reference to its Lord in these Servant Songs of Isaiah. "This was to fulfill what was spoken," Matthew repeats, and we know from our position on this side of Easter who this gentle and persistent servant really is. Like His Father, Jesus illustrates most dramatically that talk is cheap. He doesn't talk love. He does it. To Him is given the title "Word" (John 1) because He so embodies the love of God that is seen in service that His very nature reveals God. In the healings, feedings, forgivings, restorings, and, finally, in His own dying, Jesus offers Himself as the Servant of God and the model of service for God's people forever.

The section from Matthew 12 quoted above is preceded by Jesus' healing of the man with a paralyzed hand. The Pharisees are outraged because Jesus has broken the law in order to restore a broken being. In the midst of the healing and restoration, Matthew makes an almost off-hand remark. You can miss it if you're not careful: "Then the Pharisees left and made plans to kill Jesus." Then, when Jesus hears about the plotting, He merely continues to do what He has always done. He continues to serve. He quietly, unobtrusively heals and then insists that the secret be kept—for now. The full impact of the servant/healer's ministry will be known when the stone is rolled away. It will take the announcement of the angel and the resurrection of One who was declared dead in order for all of this healing to make sense. Who is Jesus? He is God's servant, and His service is crowned with glory and victory.

It is characteristic of our Lord that His service is single-minded. From the moment of His announcement in Nazareth's synagogue ("The Spirit of the Lord is on Me" [Luke 4:18]) until He commended His Spirit to the Father on the cross (Luke 23:46), Jesus was absolutely sure of His mission. He was to do what no other could do because no other had been sent by the Father to serve in such a saving way.

The Serving Christ and the Servants of Christ

What does it mean to us to know that our Lord is also our servant? He is the servant of His Father to be sure, but He still serves those who should, by all rights, be serving Him. Some might find that picture of Christ the servant an objectionable image. We would prefer to find Him seated at the right hand of the Father with a scepter in one hand and a globe in the other. Instead, we find Him kneeling at the side of a paralytic, holding a withered hand while the Pharisees hold kangaroo court.

The portrait of Jesus as servant forces us to come to grips with the most scandalous of God's realities—that God descended into the most painful parts of our world in order to serve the weak and the helpless and the oppressed. God descended to be served by a virgin peasant girl, a confused carpenter, an unknowing innkeeper, and a field of illiterate shepherds. They are working people—servants all! He takes on their flesh and yours and mine, and in so doing, glorifies the gritty task of service. His service of the lowest people, the most despised of the world, may just imply that we who are His body by Baptism might serve likewise.

But how distasteful that is to us! We would prefer to keep Him high and enthroned with cherubim and seraphim because we are so uncomfortable with Him kneeling at our feet. It is also distasteful because we (rightly) suspect that we might spend some time on our knees before the same kind of people as He served.

In the film "Baptism—The Sacrament of Belonging," a little boy, Alfredo, hideously disfigured by a fire which killed his parents, wanders homeless throughout the farm villages of Mexico. He knocks at doors asking the peasants to take him in and care for him. But when they see his scarred face, they cover their mouths and slam the doors. In his wandering, he finds an orphanage run by a group of Catholic priests. From a safe distance, he watches the joyous community of children laughing and playing, and he aches to be a part of that family. The priest in charge meets him and wants to take him into the community, but he doesn't know whether the children will accept one so grotesquely burned. The priest leaves it to the children to decide. In a beautifully moving scene, the little boy stands before the assembled group of orphans for what seems an eternity of silence as they stare at this child so severely disfigured. Then a small boy steps from the crowd to say to Alfredo, "You are my brother," and Alfredo is received into the community. It is a moment of rare insight into the meaning of the Gospel and Church and Baptism and acceptance.

When this film was shown at one confirmation retreat, however, the confirmands were not so moved by the message of the film as by anger toward God who had allowed Alfredo to be burned. Why can't we accept and love and serve those in this world who bear the scars of life under the curse of Adam? Why do we instead serve only those who bring immediate gratification to us? That's the uncomfortable question that Christ the servant would raise for us. It's not so much that we don't want to serve, it's just that we'd like to have some say as to whom we serve, when we serve, and how we're going to serve.

Whom We Serve

We'd like to serve those people who will be appropriately thankful, who, if they will not reward us immediately, will at least have the courtesy to remember our sacrifice and be eternally grateful to us.

A television episode of the seventies sitcom *Lou Grant* portrayed Rossi following a Roman Catholic sister/social worker on her rounds delivering "meals on wheels" to the elderly poor of Los Angeles. In one cramped apartment, an old man complained harshly of the bland diet he was receiving, and the sister quietly assured him that she would take his concerns to the officials. When Rossi remarked about the man's lack of gratitude, the sister explained that old people often feel very powerless and that one way of exerting authority is by complaint. She served not only through the food she delivered but as she listened to the old man complain about her work! Were the social worker less than a true servant, the old man could have starved to death.

When we look at our style of service, we notice that too often we serve only those who allow us to either feel or look good. We forget that of the ten lepers Jesus cured (Luke 17) only one returned to give thanks. Granted, Jesus expressed some wonder or disappointment, but He didn't stop serving. My response, most likely, would have been to mark lepers off as bad serving risks. I might even have revoked the cure on the other nine. (I get nasty when folk don't say "thanks!") Fortunately, God shows no such pettiness. Grace is that quality of undeserved mercy that raises a cross for the likes of you and me and that will serve on the basis of need, not payoff. The question before us is always "Why am I serving?" Is it out of an anticipated return—money, gratitude, a favor to be collected in the future—or out of guilt or fear or the expectation of approval? The answer, of course, falls into one of those categories or a myriad of others. We are, after all, only human. Human beings have a way of asking, "What's in it for me?" It will do us no good to add a burden of guilt onto the backs of the servant by asking, "Why?"

Yet it is necessary to see the ultimate reason for serving others rooted in the cross; because we have been served by our Lord, we offer up our service to Him through others. Service is responsory. Those nasty questions of payoff keep coming back to us. But as we recognize them and recognize how we shape our service to suit our needs, we are better able to risk in our service as our Lord did. We can serve those people by meeting their needs instead of shaping our service to please ourselves.

The timing of our service is another barrier to Christlike serving. I want to serve others when I'm good and ready. Every parish pastor has the experience of calls for help at the most awkward of times. During dinner, the last chapter of the great novel, the climatic scene of the television drama, or as your child is pouring out his or her soul over some trouble, the phone rings. Someone needs serving. They need serving right then, and they have some specific ideas as to how you can serve. To call them back when it is more convenient for you often negates the need for service.

In the Gospels, Jesus is portrayed as one who seeks silence and solitude, indeed needs that silence, but is constantly being interrupted. He is alone praying, and the crowds press upon Him. He goes home to His family, and the demands for His services are so great that His family thinks He's crazy (Mark 3:20–21)! Jesus knows that there is no single good time to serve because all time is dedicated to service. Every moment, if we are open to it, is a possible opportunity to share in Christ's work of service. That moment must be seized! To say to a despondent friend, "I don't have time to talk with you now," is saying really that the friend is not significant enough to replace another obligation. The parent who tells the child that "Now is not a good time to talk" had best be ready to suggest another time. I recall my younger daughter shaking her head sadly once after I had put her off. "I guess it isn't important," she said as she walked outside to play. Our call to serve comes at God's time, not our own. In the Greek language, there is a word—*kairos*—for such time. It's the opportune moment, the appointed hour. It's not a handy way of marking off moments but itself is the moment given by God in which His activity and our activity are joined together. "There is a time for everything, and a season for every activity under heaven," sings the author of Ecclesiastes (3:1). The time for service is now.

How to Serve

Our Lord also shows us how to serve. It is always to build up the one in need of service. That seems so obvious, except (as we've noted before) that a lot of service can be for the benefit of the servant. It's also necessary for the servant to know the real service that needs to be performed, and sometimes that is not what the individual to be served has in mind. In one episode of *M*A*S*H* a wounded soldier is wheeled into the operating room complaining of intense pain and asking for another shot of morphine. BJ warns him about the danger of morphine addiction, but the man insists. As he walks away, BJ notices that the man is instantly relaxing. He challenges the soldier, "You were in here just last week, and we gave you morphine then too, and your wound is not that serious. I think you're addicted to morphine." The conclusion to the story has BJ maintaining an all-night vigil with the wounded soldier while he sweats his way out of the morphine addiction.

The stated need for service and the real service required are two different matters, and the awful task facing the servant in so many situations is knowing what service to render. Here is where the Christian servant parts company from the popular image of the servant as mindless lackey. We do not react with a perfunctory nod of the head and an automatic shuffle of the feet. Instead, we are called to be so sensitive to the ones we serve that we serve their best interest, even if that is not what they always ask us to do.

That runs the risk of rejection. Parents who have attempted to serve their children's best interests can be seen as rigid and antiquated. Friends who will ask to be served in ways that hurt their health will see us as judgmental and selfish. (Because one eighteen-year-old friend of mine would not buy his underage friends beer from the local store, he was frozen out of their social circle.)

But then we serve in the name of Christ who made some decisions about how He served as well. The Zealots wanted revolution, and the Pharisees expected legalistic conformity. Pilate wanted peace and quiet, and the masses wanted bread. Jesus served on His terms, which were the Father's terms, and for that He was crucified. We do not serve as others tell us to, but as our Lord directs. In that service, we find exhilarating freedom. We also find that God uses that service to build up His people in ways that they would never believe possible.

Christlike Service

Can we serve as Christ served? Of course not. But that doesn't stop us from keeping Him as our model and our power. We remember those strange words about finding Him in the hungry, thirsty, naked, imprisoned, and lonely (Matthew 25). Since we know we serve Him in serving others, we serve others in His name. Our "why" is seen in the cross, the "who" is all whom He served, the "when" is now, and the "how" is through prayerful reflection on their condition. We must serve as we have been served.

THE WAY OF THE SERVANT

DISCUSSION QUESTIONS ON THE SECOND READING

1. How is Jesus the Word? What functions do words play? What have your words done today? How were your words like Jesus, the Word of God?

2. What work that you have done recently mirrors Jesus' work? (Come on now, get creative.)

3. What feelings do you get when others refuse to thank you for the work you do? How do you respond to their thanklessness?

4. What payoff did you receive for the work you did today? Was it sufficient to motivate better work tomorrow? If not, why? What payoff do you need to keep you going?

5. How have you expressed your gratitude to one who has served you today? Do you want to do it now? (Go ahead and do it.)

6. Think of an example from your life recently when what you were asked to do was not really the service that was required?

Servant Studies © 2007 Concordia Publishing House. Okay to copy.

THE THIRD READING: THE SERVANT SPIRIT

> I believe that I cannot by my own reason or strength believe in Jesus Christ, my Lord, or come to Him; but the Holy Spirit has called me by the Gospel, enlightened me with His gifts, sanctified and kept me in the true faith. In the same way He calls, gathers, enlightens, and sanctifies the whole Christian church on earth. (Martin Luther's explanation of the Third Article)

In Colorado Springs, Colorado, there is a remarkable retreat center. It's called Glen Eyrie and is owned by the Navigators, an evangelistic organization. Years ago, a railroad magnate built this striking castle in the wilderness as a sign of civilization in the unsettled West. He had traveled to Europe and brought the plans back with him. General Palmer had quite a retinue of servants, and he designed his castle so that his servants could move quickly and efficiently around the building in complete silence. Secret passageways, hidden staircases, disguised panels that are really doors—all open with the push of a button to allow servants to slip unnoticed about the large building.

The good servant knows that he or she is to be seldom seen and never heard. God the Spirit is such a silent servant. The Spirit's sound is a whisper like a breath of the wind blowing through the branches of a tree. He shakes leaves and boughs, rattles a wind chime or two, but the calling, enlightening, sanctifying, and later gathering are all activities of a silent Spirit—a servant Spirit.

Luther describes the activities of God the Spirit with serving words. The calling is a gracious invitation to citizenship in God's kingdom. The infant over the font may stretch its new lungs to the breaking point and turn bluer than the water in the bowl, but the Spirit's call is silent. The enlightening of God's people seldom comes with crashing clarity or the cartoonist's lightbulb. It is usually formed over long years of living life and noticing God's gracious ways of working through the common stuff around us. The sanctifying, that is, "making holy," is accompanied in some church bodies with whoops and hollers, shouts of joy, and ecstatic utterance. But for most of us, it's so quiet that we're not always sure it's being done

God the silent servant is so intent on breathing new life into His people that we are often not aware of His presence. In the movie *Oh, God!* a frustrated store clerk portrayed by John Denver asks God (played by George Burns) why He isn't more direct in revealing Himself to humanity. Why not a few well-placed miracles?

"I don't do miracles," God says with a smile. "Too flashy." We share the store clerk's frustration, don't we? Why not a miraculous healing for the lingering cancer patient in the hospice? How about an easy zap of bliss for the couple intent on destroying their marriage before their kids reach puberty? Let's see instant employment for the out-of-work and an easy cure for the alcoholic and drug addict.

What He does do—and He does it well—is calling, enlightening, sanctifying, and gathering. He serves us, this silent Spirit, in whispers and sighs by moving through the hearts and minds of His people, thus making them His miracles to others. We who are the servants of Christ are used by Him to accomplish His purpose of calling, gathering, enlightening, and sanctifying. The marvel of it all is that while we are in His service, He is serving us in those same ways.

Calling Servants

A servant of God is one who is constantly calling others to closer fellowship with their Father and His Son. We normally term this service *evangelism*, but once we label it, package it, and turn it over to some committee we forget that all service in the name of Christ is evangelism. Yet, service is seductive. Once you've been served well, you find that you want to know more about the servant—what makes him or her tick? Why does the servant do what he or she does? Why did Mother Theresa spend all that time and energy serving people who would never return the favor, who could never offer service to her? Then when you hear her say something about Christ being in those people and Christ calling her to serve them, you notice the tear in the corner of your eye and you feel strangely drawn, not to Mother Theresa, but to the Christ who has drawn her. You have been called by God through one of His servants, and you begin to suspect that maybe He can call others through you. There are words sometimes: words of Christ and salvation and Gospel and such religious themes. Often, though, there are none. You merely do the service and hope that someone senses Christ's hand through yours. The Silent Servant whispers in what you do. Others will sense it—don't doubt it!

Enlightening Servants

As servants of the Spirit of God we are called to enlighten. There is a kind of mystic quality about enlightening. One person has some secret that he or she shares with another, who in turn shares it with another, and on down the chain until all of us little folk get enlightened too. Most contemporary gurus put a price tag on such enlightening—and there seems to be no shortage of those who will pay the bill.

The enlightening of the Spirit, though, is nothing mystic. At the time when the infant Church was being formed, a group of quasi-Christians called Gnostics claimed that they held the enlightening secret that others could find only through participation in their secret rituals and ways. Paul fought a continuous battle with these first-century cultists by claiming that there really was nothing all that secret about the Christian religion. It was given to us by God through Christ Jesus. God's Spirit gave everyone specific gifts for service (I Corinthians 12), and if you want to know the "most excellent way," try love (I Corinthians 13)—that's all. Love: no gooey or mushy feeling, this quality of enlightenment that Paul commends for us, but the undergirding to all of life within the Christian community. The lights are turned on in our darkened lives by the love of God in Christ Jesus. We, in turn, so lighten others through the same love.

How is this love shown? By the very specific, menial ways that we serve them in love. It bothers me to see I Corinthians 13 (the "love chapter" of poetic note) reproduced on some greeting card in a Christian gift shop as though it could stand apart from the implementation of that love through service. Embroider it on a workman's glove. Carve it on the dashboard of your pickup. Print it into the fabric of a dish towel. Then you've got the living chapter. As a static piece of art primly placed on some display rack, it's a sleeper.

To enlighten your neighbor in the most meaningful way, serve him or her. The best service might be a few words that let him or her know that there is more to life than bread and circuses, but remember that words are only the beginning. You are your neighbor's enlightenment in word and action, and God will give you the power for that enlightening.

Sanctifying Servants

The little church of which I am pastor is no more than a small meeting room set into the side of a hill in southeast Denver, Colorado. Those who seek a cathedral walk in one door and out the other. The church down the road is named Shepherd of the Hills, so my waggish wife calls our situation God in the Sod. (We really are built into the side of a hill!) Still, there is a strong feeling among our membership that this little underground chapel is holy ground. With no stained glass or pitched roof or architectural magnificence, we know that we are in church and are Church when we gather for worship. The reason for that is that holiness is best understood as being set apart for a purpose. When God's servant Spirit sanctifies, He sets apart His people for the purpose of worshiping and serving God. There is no mass distribution of halos to God's own, only servant's aprons. Our glory is in our service, not in some aloof sanctity that sets us apart from the standards of a self-centered world.

Gathered Servants

Finally, the Spirit gathers the servants together into the Church. We are a network of servants, washing one another's feet and reaching out from our own circles to serve the world. Those in the baptized fellowship of servants know that their service is multiplied as they enlist others in service, training, preparing "for works of service" (Ephesians 4:12), and remembering alongside one another our mutual ministries. The gathered company of servants knows that ministry performed alone is exhausting and often discouraging. We need one another in our serving. Even Jesus chose a company of servants; dare we do any less? The congregation is a gift of the Spirit to individual servants to let them know that they never serve alone. We are together the Body of Christ and, therefore, are members one of another.

Serving in the Name of the Spirit

It is a quiet ministry, often with little reward or recognition, for that is the nature of the Spirit's service. God's Spirit chooses to work through others and, therefore, the Spirit surrenders His glory. The Sacraments of Baptism and the Lord's Supper are the most common events in the congregation's life, yet they are God's service to us through His Holy Spirit. God's Word in Scripture is more often argued about than seen for what it is—the vehicle of His service. So when we serve in the name of the Spirit of God without visible recognition or reward, we only carry on His service. While we are calling, gathering, enlightening, and sanctifying through service, we are the recipients of the Spirit's service to us. Through Word, Sacrament, and gathered Body of the sanctified we are nourished in our service.

THE WAY OF THE SERVANT

DISCUSSION QUESTIONS ON THE THIRD READING

1. Can you think of some of the less flashy miracles of God that you saw today?

2. How does service make itself seductive? When were you seduced into service?

3. What in your work today enlightened you as to the meaning of God's working grace in this world?

4. The Spirit gathers His servants. Are these gatherings only in authorized congregations? Where do the servants of Christ gather? How has your gathering, your group of servants in which you are now participating, strengthened you for service?

Servant Studies © 2007 Concordia Publishing House. Okay to copy.

THE FOURTH READING: THE MAN WHO WOULD NOT BE SERVED

"THE SECRET OF THE SERVANT'S BOWL."

> He came to Simon Peter, who said to Him, "Lord, are you going to wash my feet?" Jesus replied, "You do not realize now what I am doing, but later you will understand." "No," said Peter, "You shall never wash my feet." Jesus answered, "Unless I wash you, you have no part with Me." (John 13:6–8)

Simon, Simon, simple Simon, don't you understand?

Will you ever understand?

Taking off His coat, rolling up His sleeves, wrapping the apron around His waist like some short-order cook instead of the Lord of all creation.

Don't you know what He is doing?

So *indignant* you sound, so pompous and put out as He kneels before you.

Really, Jesus, wash *my* feet?

Never . . . ever . . . 'til the end of the close of the age. (It'll be a cold day in the kingdom when my feet meet Your basin.)

Well, bluster on, little man. You must have found Him insulting, Peter. A little tacky maybe?

After all, He is the Christ, the Son of the living God. You said so, and in His smile you knew that you were right.

He agreed with you.

Ah . . . the satisfaction of showing all those others who you were. You were of the inner circle of the Christ,

The Son of the living God.

You may have been a hick fisherman on Galilee's fickle lake, but now you knew the Christ and He knew you.

He even called you by name, a new name: "Peter," "Cephas," "The Rock"—on your words of faith would be built the Church.

From simple Simon to "The Rock." Hmmm, a nice ring to it.

Not bad for a hick fisherman from the fickle lake of Galilee. You would regale the boys on the dock with wonder stories

Of His miracles—the healings and the feeding (5,000 in one sitting). Of the Roman centurion who came *to Him* for a curing and of the fishermen who would sit with eyes wide and mouths open for they knew too:

He was the Christ, the Son of the living God.

Even your wife looked on you with new respect, didn't she? Ever since that day, hot and sticky, when her mother lay sweating and writhing on the couch and with just the touch of His hand on hers . . . gone the fever and the sweat and the pain.

Remember how you felt as you left the house? All eyes followed Him . . . and you, "Simon." You heard them ask in unbelief, "Simon bar-Jonah with the rabbi?" Such respect was yours, Peter, such respect.

And in spite of all His words, His stories of service, you yet believed that He would fight and win and the world would know that you were on the team of the winner.

Let James and John argue about who would be the first in the Kingdom; You knew that you'd be there first—marching in the front of the parade as Israel proclaimed Him King Christ, Son of the living God.

Simon, Simon, simple Simon. Don't you understand? Will you ever understand? Maybe now that the King has taken off His coat and rolled up the sleeves with your big, calloused foot in His lap. As He kneels before you. Now you may know what it means to be free. To be free to serve as freely as He.

He says it for you. Of course you don't know. Not now. Not yet. But wait. Wait awhile.

Wait until the garden is still and the angry echoes fill the halls of the Sanhedrin.

Wait until the crack of the lash is quiet, the final sentence pronounced.

Wait until the three accusing crows of the cock have faded into the dawn. And wait until the creaking of the cross has ceased.

Wait until all is finished, completed, accomplished,

Then run!

Run, Peter, to the tomb at the word of a woman.

Run to see the linen lying. Run on feet that He has washed clean, as He will wash you clean to the core. Forever.

Run to know *then* what it is that He knows now.

"I serve you in a wet way, Peter," He says, washing, slowly,

Deliberately, "so that I can give to you the towel and basin, the apron and ewer. And you will wash the world's feet."

So all of us who by baptismal water are built upon this reluctant rock

Are given the Spirit's flood, the word to wash and serve the Lord. By seeing those He died to save.

The towel and basin, ewer and apron, come to us

As a cleansing kit, and He sends us from His empty cross,

From His tomb of joyous vacancy, out to look for feet to wash.

For now we know, on this side of Easter, the meaning Peter could not know: that we are saved and served by a risen Christ who gives great glory to the act of washing, serving.

To be the greatest is to be the servant at the feet of a very dirty world indeed.

The tired feet of a welfare mother and the crippled feet of the Gulf War vet,

The cloth-wrapped feet of the worker waiting in line for a bit of bread—all are there for us to wash as once He washed His disciples' feet.

He whose feet were pierced, not washed,

Whose feet walked shakily, but surely, from tomb to Easter ground. "You do not know, Peter, but later you will understand."

Now *we* know, like simple Simon. In our ears we hear the "Feed My Sheep" and "Wash their feet," but we forget in our hearts,

Which is why we pray for Your Spirit, Lord, the one who blows the water's waves,

Who blew creation's waters down and hovered over Jordan's stream,

Who blessed our old baptismal bowl, to make us live and love and dream. Send now Your water/wind upon this bowl,

That each of us washed clean by You may scrub the world's wounds and woes and wash Your people clean again. Give us the grace to know the secret of the servant's bowl.

Amen.

THE WAY OF THE SERVANT

DISCUSSION QUESTIONS ON THE FOURTH READING

1. Read the account of the foot washing in **John 13** (the whole chapter). How would you have reacted were you in Peter's place?

2. Have you ever had your feet washed? Discuss your feelings. How about a shoe shine? Do you recall how you felt about the person shining your shoes?

Servant Studies © 2007 Concordia Publishing House. Okay to copy.

Notes for the Leader

The group could be gathered together in a secluded place either indoors or outdoors on four evenings for the oral reading of "The Way of the Servant" by several fluent readers. Discussion should follow or copies could be made for each participant to read and reflect on silently prior to a group discussion.

The conclusion of the readings might be a good time for a foot washing. It is a simple ceremony that some churches find meaningful on Maundy Thursday. Lighting in the room should be subdued to allow for a peaceful spirit of meditation. A cross should be the focal point with a basin, ewer of warm water, and towel placed in the center of the chairs.

If you group is small, the leader might wish to wash the feet of everyone. In larger gatherings, a representative group is often chosen (twelve is often the number, symbolic of the disciples). The foot washing should be slow and unhurried. During the washing, John 13 should be read. See the "Order for the Washing of Feet" in the Worship Resources section.

5

WORSHIP RESOURCES

Worship and related events are a vital part of extended Servant Events. The resources that follow include orders for the opening and closing of service events, as well as litanies for use throughout the week. The "Order for the Washing of Feet" is especially appropriate for use at the conclusion of a week of service.

WORSHIP AT THE START OF A SERVANT EVENT

A Note to the Leader

Congratulations! You survived the first night! Now the first morning may be another story. We will begin by calling on the name of the Lord who made heaven and earth. His creative activity is important for us to recall this morning. Your crew of servants may, for a variety of reasons, be anxious about the task at hand. This worship experience is designed to comfort you with the good news that God is a marvelous builder who uses things as simple as dirt (remember Adam?) and cubits (is that a metric measurement?) to achieve His masterpieces. You have placed yourselves into His hands. He will build wonderful things through you. Praise His name!

HOLY HOUSEMAKERS

The Opening Hymn:
"Awake, My Soul, and with the Sun" (*LSB* 868; *LW* 478) or "Greet the Rising Sun" (*LSB* 871; *HS98* 902)

The Invocation:

Leader:	We are here
People:	**With hearts** (*Touch your chest.*)
	And hands (*Stick them in the air and shake them.*)
	And voices (*Chant "we're here God" four times.*)
Leader:	To break our backs and our pride in the service of God,
People:	**The Father, Son, and Holy Spirit.**
Leader:	Amen.
People:	**Hallelujah!**

The Prayer:

Leader:	The Lord be with you.
People:	**May He be with you too.**
Leader:	Let us pray.
All:	**Almighty God, our Father, You have set before us a new day filled with challenge and opportunity. Strengthen us by Your Holy Spirit that we might fulfill our tasks with joy and glorify Your holy name through Jesus Christ, our Lord, who lives and reigns with You and the Holy Spirit, ever one God. Amen.**

The Reading:
Luke 4:16–22

The Meditation:
Jesus Is a Carpenter

Chances are good your group may have a whole lot more enthusiasm than experience about the task. That could cause a great deal of anxiety. That's why it's important to remember that the Lord we serve here was and is a carpenter. That's what the people of Nazareth found so astounding when He spoke those gracious words. "Isn't this Joseph's son?" they asked. They all knew that carpenter's sons seldom became learned in that day and age. Yes, Jesus is our learned Lord. He is the very wisdom of God. However, today we want to remember that He is a carpenter.

Jesus knows how to lay out jobs, gather materials, drive nails, cut boards, and sand finishes. Jesus also knows how wonderfully close you become to people you work with. He's done it all before, and now His Spirit rests upon us.

That Spirit will guide us as we measure and saw, lift and carry. He'll grant us the benefit of His experience. He has called us to this work, and He won't abandon us. Instead, He'll shower us with every gift we need to get the job done to His glory.

When we get tired, He'll give us His strength. When we're not sure what to do, He'll give us instruction. When our patience runs out, He'll give us His own patience.

It was once said of Jesus, "He does all things well." It will be said of Him again by those who see our work this week. Jesus, by whose death and resurrection our sins are forgiven and who even now is building a mansion for us in heaven, will bless our building, too, so that we can be blessings to the world.

The Prayers:

Leader: Lord, we lift our hands before You.

People: Take a good look at them, Lord; they won't be like this much longer.

Leader: In a moment, Father,

People: They'll get bruised, maybe cut, dirty, perhaps even painted,

Leader: For You

People: As a way to say "thank You," for all You have done for us in Jesus Christ, our Savior and Brother and Carpenter Friend.

Leader: If sin tears us down today . . .

People: Jesus, use Your powerful hands to build us up.

Leader: If we get rough with each other . . .

People: Sand us down with Your love, Jesus, and make us smooth.

Leader: If we become prideful or boastful . . .

People: Jesus, cut us down to size so we'll fit in Your kingdom.

Leader: Keep us from all danger.

People: Send Your angels to protect us.

Leader: May all that we do glorify Your name.

People: Amen.

The Blessing:

Leader: May the Lord watch over your hammering and nailing, your painting and sanding, your laughing and crying on this day and all your days, and may the blessing of God, the Father, Son, and Holy Spirit, be yours forever.

People: **Amen.**

Leader: Go in peace; serve the Lord.

People: **Thanks be to God.**

The Closing Hymn:
"With the Lord Begin Your Task" (*LSB* 869; *LW* 483; *TLH* 540)

HOLY HOUSEMAKERS

The Opening Hymn:
"Awake, My Soul, and with the Sun" (*LSB* 868; *LW* 478) or "Greet the Rising Sun" (*LSB* 871; *HS98* 902)

The Invocation:
Leader: We are here

People: With hearts (*Touch your chest.*)

And hands (*Stick them in the air and shake them.*)

And voices (*Chant "we're here God" four times.*)

Leader: To break our backs and our pride in the service of God,

People: The Father, Son, and Holy Spirit.

Leader: Amen.

People: Hallelujah!

The Prayer:
Leader: The Lord be with you.

People: May He be with you too.

Leader: Let us pray.

All: Almighty God, our Father, You have set before us a new day filled with challenge and opportunity. Strengthen us by Your Holy Spirit that we might fulfill our tasks with joy and glorify Your holy name through Jesus Christ, our Lord, who lives and reigns with You and the Holy Spirit, ever one God. Amen.

The Reading: Luke 4:16–22

The Meditation: *Jesus Is a Carpenter*

The Prayers:

Leader: Lord, we lift our hands before You.

People: Take a good look at them, Lord; they won't be like this much longer.

Leader: In a moment, Father,

People: They'll get bruised, maybe cut, dirty, perhaps even painted,

Leader: For You

People: As a way to say "thank You" for all You have done for us in Jesus Christ, our Savior and Brother and Carpenter Friend.

Leader: If sin tears us down today . . .

People: Jesus use Your powerful hands to build us up.

Leader: If we get rough with each other . . .

People: Sand us down with Your love, Jesus, and make us smooth.

Leader: If we become prideful or boastful . . .

People: Jesus, cut us down to size so we'll fit in Your kingdom.

Leader: Keep us from all danger.

People: Send Your angels to protect us.

Leader: May all that we do glorify Your name.

People: Amen.

The Blessing:

Leader: May the Lord watch over your hammering and nailing, your painting and sanding, your laughing and crying on this day and all your days, and may the blessing of God, the Father, Son, and Holy Spirit be yours forever.

People: Amen.

Leader: Go in peace; serve the Lord.

People: Thanks be to God.

The Closing Hymn: "With the Lord Begin Your Task" (*LSB* 869; *LW* 483; *TLH* 540)

Servant Studies © 2007 Concordia Publishing House. Okay to copy.

CLOSING WORSHIP

Opening Hymn

"Lord, Whose Love through Humble Service" (*LSB* 848; *HS98* 882)

A Servant Psalm

The following poem/prayer traces the serving ministry of our Lord as reported in Matthew's Gospel. The groups should be divided up into three sections for the reading.

All: Bless the Lord Jesus, the servant of all.

Group 1: The lepers came for cleansing . . .

Group 2: He touched them into wholeness.

Group 1: A servant, near to dying . . .

Group 2: He spoke a word, gave healing.

Group 1: Peter's mother-in-law so fevered . . .

Group 2: A touch—she's back to serving.

Group 3: Demon possessed, possessed no more, a paralytic walks the floor, and sinners sit at table.

All: Bless the Lord Jesus, the servant of all.

Group 1: "My daughter, Lord, is dead now . . ."

Group 2: They're gasping! She is living!

Group 1: The woman grasps His garment . . .

Group 2: Instantly she's healed!

Group 1: Blind men cry, "Have mercy!"

Group 2: They see and tell His story.

Group 3: Tongues unstopped can speak His praise, twelve disciples walk His ways—all servants, like their Master.

All: Bless the Lord Jesus, the servant of all.

Group 1: A withered hand, stretched out, restored . . .

Group 2: May follow—healed and joyful.

Group 1: A Canaanite woman cries for help . . .

Group 2: "Great is your faith, come into the Kingdom!"

Group 1: More than four thousand fed with so little . . .

Group 2: Fish and bread and so much left over.

Group 3: "You are the Christ. And so I must die." Transfigured on a mountain high, and back on the plain, He's healing.

All: Bless the Lord Jesus, the servant of all.

Group 1: They bring the children to be touched . . .

Group 2: A rich man leaves Him, grieving.

Group 1: A blind man cries by the side of the road . . .

Group 2: He follows the servant, now seeing.

Group 1: The lame and the blind in the temple, all healed . . .

Group 2: "Hosanna to the Son of David!"

Group 3: Betrayed and tried and crucified, in resurrection glorified. "Go make disciples, serving!"

All: Bless the Lord Jesus! Yes! Our Lord Jesus! We are the servants of all!

Prayers

Prayers may be offered

* in thanksgiving for the Lord's ministry;

* for strength to serve as He did; and

* for specific concerns of the day;

The Creed Seals Our Day

I believe in God, the Father Almighty,
   Maker of heaven and earth.
And in Jesus Christ, His only Son, our Lord,
   who was conceived by the Holy Spirit,
   born of the virgin Mary.
   suffered under Pontius Pilate,
   was crucified, died and was buried.
   He descended into hell.
   The third day He rose again from the dead.
   He ascended into heaven
   and sits at the right hand of God, the Father Almighty.
   From thence He will come to judge the living and the dead.
I believe in the Holy Spirit,
   the holy Christian church,
       the communion of saints,
   the forgiveness of sins,
   the resurrection of the body,
   and the life everlasting. Amen.

The Evening Prayer of Dr. Luther

I thank You, my heavenly Father, through Jesus Christ, Your dear Son, that You have graciously kept me this day; and I pray that You would forgive me all my sins where I have done wrong, and graciously keep me this night. For into Your hands I commend myself, my body and soul, and all things. Let Your holy angel be with me, that the evil foe may have no power over me. Amen.

A Benediction

Leader: May our almighty Lord—Father, Son, and Holy Spirit—grant us a quiet night and peace at the last.

All: Amen!

Servant Studies © 2007 Concordia Publishing House. *Luther's Small Catechism with Explanation* © 1986, 1991 Concordia Publishing House. Okay to copy.

RESPONSIVE LITANY FOR THE START OF A SERVANT EVENT

Leader: Gracious God, we thank You for safely bringing us to this place. Keep us safe during the coming week. Lord, in Your mercy . . .

Servants: Hear our prayer.

Leader: Lord, we come from different backgrounds, different parts of the country, and different congregations. Help us to appreciate those differences and our unity in Christ Jesus, who through His death and resurrection has made one all who believe in Him. Lord, in Your mercy . . .

Servants: Hear our prayer.

Leader: We are here to serve You, Father. Help us to give You glory in all that we do. Lord, in Your mercy . . .

Servants: Hear our prayer.

Leader: There is much work to do. There are many tasks to be done. O Lord Jesus, give us strength and courage. Lord, in Your mercy . . .

Servants: Hear our prayer.

Leader: We thank You for the new friends we have met here. Help us to continue to build those relationships and grow closer to You in the process. Lord, in Your mercy . . .

Servants: Hear our prayer.

Leader: Now, Father, give us a restful night that we may arise refreshed and renewed to begin a new day of service in Your name. Lord, in Your mercy . . .

Servants: Hear our prayer. Amen.

Servant Studies © 2007 Concordia Publishing House. Okay to copy.

RESPONSIVE LITANY FOR THE CLOSE OF A SERVANT EVENT

Leader: Heavenly Father, we thank You for safely bringing us to the close of this Servant Event. We ask You to continue to bless us on our journey.

People: Be with us in our travels as we return home to our families and friends.

Leader: Father, we especially thank You for the new friends we have made here.

People: Help us to show care and love to those new acquaintances.

Leader: Lord, You have taught us much during our service.

People: Help us to continue to grow in our understanding of our role in this world.

Leader: Thank You, Father, for the example of Your Son, who lived among us and who showed us how to care.

People: Allow us to be "little Christs" to those around us in all we do.

Leader: Be with those who remain here after we go.

People: Assist them in this mission and allow them to be a blessing to others.

Leader: On behalf of this community, I speak words to you servants: "Well done, you good and faithful servants." I now commission you to go out in the world, sharing what you have learned, caring for those in your community, and bearing the burdens of others in the name of the Father and the Son and the Holy Spirit. Amen.

Servant Studies © 2007 Concordia Publishing House. Okay to copy.

A LITANY OF THE SERVED

Leader: We gather as servants but also as those who have been so richly served. We thank You, God for our servants! For those this day who have been Your ministers in our life. For those near and those far.

Servants: For all Your servants, we thank You, Lord!

L: For parents and loved ones far away whose sacrifices, commitment to us, and prayers have brought us to this time.

S: For Your servants—our parents and loved ones—we thank You, Lord!

L: For public servants—our guardians and protectors. For the president of the United States and the governor and public servants of this state. For all of those who work to keep order and to protect us.

S: For public servants who minister in Your creation, we thank You, Lord!

L: We thank You for artists, musicians, and craftspeople; for preparers of food, writers, poets, and all who tend and direct the beauty of Your beautiful world.

S: For all those who enrich our life through art and craft, we thank You, Lord!

L: And for this gathering of servants. For the ways, known and unknown, in which we serve one another. We thank You for the gifts, talents, and abilities You have given us, but chiefly for the love of Your Son that moves us to serve one another. (We can offer thanks for specific persons and for their gifts of service over the past week.) Grant us the grace, Lord, to be served by others as by You. Help us always to know that Your service of us comes to us by others. Let us receive Your servants as we receive You.

S: Grant us grace to be served, Lord. Amen.

Servant Studies © 2007 Concordia Publishing House. Okay to copy.

SERVANT HEART PRAYER WALK

Just as prayer is a part of our daily life, it can also be an important part of your time of service. These prayer opportunities are designed to be used in a variety of settings. Your church sanctuary, fellowship hall, or youth room can be the location for this prayer walk designed to give youth a quiet time to reflect on the opportunities God provides in our lives for service to others.

You'll need:

Large room with permanent altar or one you have created yourself

6–12 Bibles

Seating or chairs for twelve people

Printed copies of the study

PRAYER WALK STATION 1

"FOR I WAS HUNGRY AND YOU GAVE ME SOMETHING TO EAT."
MATTHEW 25:35A

Millions of people go hungry each day. For them, a small portion of bread or rice is a gourmet meal.

Millions of people are also starving for the bread of life, Jesus Christ. Jesus tells us in John 6:35, "I am the bread of life. He who comes to Me will never go hungry."

 Think for a moment about someone you may know who is physically hungry.

 Think of someone you may know who is spiritually hungry.

 Thank God for the physical and spiritual blessings He gives you.

 Pray for those who are physically and spiritually hungry.

Servant Studies © 2007 Concordia Publishing House. Scripture: NIV®. Okay to copy.

PRAYER WALK STATION 2

"I WAS THIRSTY AND YOU GAVE ME SOMETHING TO DRINK."
MATTHEW 25:35B

There is nothing more refreshing after exhausting work than a glass of cool, fresh water. Water not only refreshes us, it sustains us.

As Jesus talked with the Samaritan woman, He told her, "Whoever drinks the water I give him will never thirst. Indeed, the water I give him will become in him a spring of water welling up to eternal life." John 4:14

 As Christians, we thirst for God's Word. It refreshes and sustains us in daily life.

 Pray that you will daily thirst for His Word and search it for new discoveries.

Servant Studies © 2007 Concordia Publishing House. Scripture: ESV®. Okay to copy.

PRAYER WALK STATION 3

"I WAS A STRANGER AND YOU INVITED ME IN." MATTHEW 25:35C

Everyone enjoys visiting a friend's home. We may be celebrating a special occasion or just stopping by for a brief visit.

Sometimes, due to our busy schedules, friends can become strangers. We neglect to communicate with them regularly and sometime lose contact with them.

We are in contact daily with many strangers. It may be someone in our school or church. It may be someone in the place where we work. It may be someone in our neighborhood or any other place we frequent. A stranger can appreciate our warm smile, our friendly greeting, or our worlds of welcome.

We read in Hebrews 13:2, "Do not forget to entertain strangers, for by so doing some people have entertained angels without knowing it."

 Think of a stranger in your life. Is it a friend you have neglected or a friend waiting to be made?

 Thank God for the people who aren't strangers in your life.

 Ask God to direct you to be open and responsive to the strangers He places in your life.

Servant Studies © 2007 Concordia Publishing House. Scripture: NIV®. Okay to copy.

PRAYER WALK STATION 4

"I NEEDED CLOTHES AND YOU CLOTHED ME." MATTHEW 25:36A

Do you have something in your closet that you no longer wear because it doesn't fit or is out of style? You probably do. There is one article in our wardrobe that never changes.

"For all of you who were baptized into Christ have clothed yourselves with Christ" (Galatians 3:27). Through our Baptism, we daily wear the garment of Christ.

 Is there someone you know who isn't baptized?

 Ask the Holy Spirit to help you share your faith and baptism promises.

 Thank God that you are clothed with the love and assurance of Christ's promises.

Servant Studies © 2007 Concordia Publishing House. Scripture: NIV®. Okay to copy.

PRAYER WALK STATION 5

"I WAS SICK AND YOU LOOKED AFTER ME." MATTHEW 25:36B

It's never fun to be sick. Very often it is even more difficult when your sickness makes it necessary to visit the doctor. Christ had many experiences with people who were sick. He often healed them and comforted them in their afflictions.

Christians can become sick. Our prayer life may be weak. We may be lax in regular "checkups" with His Word and Sacrament. Our daily dose of Bible study may be forgotten.

 Think of someone you know who is in need of God's healing hand. Ask God to restore their health.

 Confess to God those times when your Christian life has been sick and suffering. Be assured of the medicine of His forgiveness.

Servant Studies © 2007 Concordia Publishing House. Scripture: NIV®. Okay to copy.

PRAYER WALK STATION 6

"I WAS IN PRISON AND YOU CAME TO VISIT ME." MATTHEW 25:36C

You don't have to be living in a maximum security correction facility to be considered a prisoner. Many people in today's society are prisoners to alcohol, drugs, and other controlled substances. Others are prisoners to the place where they reside, such as the elderly who are left forgotten and forsaken by the families in their homes or convalescent facilities.

As Christians, we are also prisoners of sorts. We struggle with sin every day. Christ's death and resurrection frees us from being prisoners to the sin that affects our lives.

 Think of someone you know who may be a prisoner. Ask God to guide and care for him or her as he or she struggles to be free.

 Thank God for making you free from the prison of sin.

"I tell you the truth, whatever you did for one of the least of these brothers of Mine, you did for Me." Matthew 25:40

 We are Christ's disciples. Approach His altar now. Thank Him for the privilege of being His ambassador to the world. Ask Him to give you the strength and courage to meet the challenges this endeavor requires. Though a quiet time of prayer, place at the foot of His cross your cares, your worries, your burdens, and your thanksgivings.

Servant Studies © 2007 Concordia Publishing House. Scripture: NIV®. Okay to copy.

ORDER FOR THE WASHING OF FEET

The group of servants may gather in an area apart from disturbance. Lighting in the room should be subdued to allow for a peaceful spirit of meditation. A cross should be the focal point. A basin, ewer (pitcher) of warm water, and a towel should be placed on a table near the cross.

If your group is small, the leader might wish to wash the feet of everyone. In larger gatherings, a representative group is often chosen (twelve is the usual number, symbolic of the disciples). The foot washing should be slow and unhurried. The reading of John 13 may be timed to extend throughout the foot washing. Those who are to be served through the foot washing should be asked beforehand. Their shoes and socks are to be removed at the beginning of the service.

Opening Hymn

"Jesus, Greatest at the Table" (*LSB* 446) or another hymn based on our Lord's Passion or the glory of servanthood and discipleship

The Psalm: Psalm 116:12–17 (ESV)

Right side (R): What shall I render to the Lord for all His benefits to me?

Left side (L): I will lift up the cup of salvation and call on the name of the Lord.

R: I will pay my vows to the Lord in the presence of all His people.

L: Precious in the sight of the Lord is the death of His saints.

R: O Lord, I am Your servant; I am Your servant, the son of Your maidservant. You have loosed my bonds.

L: I will offer to You the sacrifice of thanksgiving, and call on the name of the Lord.

A Reading: "The Foot Servant"

"After that, He poured water into a basin and began to wash His disciples' feet." John 13:5

Feet.

So many feet in this world. Most human beings have a pair—two of them at the end of ankles, at the end of calves, at the end of knees, of thighs, of groins—but always at the end of something. Feet are the bottom line of the human body and, as such, get the worst wear.

Feet look bad.

Well, to be fair, young feet aren't all that ugly. Babies' feet are cute ("this little piggy went to the market . . ."). Teenage feet may even look okay in a pair of expensive sandals. Girls paint their toes and, recently, some buy little rings that they wrap around their toes (doesn't that make running difficult?).

Still, though you can paint your nails and ornament them to look good, most of us stick our feet away in socks and shoes at the beginning of each day for practical reasons. We hide them, not in shame, but to protect them from the dangers of the earth upon which we walk. Over the years, feet that once looked not bad get twisted and bent, callused and misshapen. There are some feet, older people's feet, that resemble claws. They are not pretty. These are the feet He held in His hands.

Feet stink.

If they're stashed away in socks and leather shoes, the bacteria forms over the day. You kick off your loafers in class, and people around you sniff the air, wondering what has died in the room. Have you ever left those socks and sweat-wet shoes in your bedroom at night with the windows closed because you're too tired to air them out? Ever carpeted your bedroom floor with a week's worth of athletic socks after soccer or baseball games? Remember how your bedroom smelled? A bad pollution day in Los Angeles or Chicago, Denver or New York would be a relief! Feet stink! These are the feet He held in His hands.

Feet hurt.

How do your feet feel now? You have been on them all day. You have climbed ladders, perhaps walked miles, and stood on them while you waited, listened, joked and prayed. You have supported all of your 130 or 180 pounds on those two things all day. Do they hurt? Wouldn't it be nice if someone picked your foot up and cradled it in the palm of His hand and let cool water run over that ugly, stinky foot while He massages it gently with His strong fingers? He did. It was hurting feet that He held in His hands.

The great philosopher Socrates, with his death only a few hours away, stirs the hemlock poison and lectures his disciples on the meaning of life. With the cross only a few hours away, Jesus of Nazareth cares for twenty-four ugly, stinking, and hurting feet. He even washed Judas's feet, knowing that soon they would trot off to the courts of the killers to turn Him in.

Jesus is doing servants' work, of course, and that's just the point. What He does on the night in which He was betrayed is no different than what He has been doing since His feet walked out of the Jordan River, wet with baptismal water. They were servants' feet then, and they are now, and soon His feet will be clamped together by a soldier's strong hands and a spike will fasten them, one on top of the other, to a vertical pole, there to bleed freely until death stops their twitching.

But for now He kneels to wash His disciples' feet and ours and to let them and us know that "now that I, your Lord and Teacher, have washed your feet, you also should wash one another's feet" (John 13:14).

Think of that the next time a friend says, "Ooooh, my feet are killing me" or "I just can't stand it anymore!" Think of their pain, and of the one who would kneel before us all as servant and Lord. Think of their feet, take one in your hand, and wash.

The Washing

As a reader reads John 13, the leader wraps an apron or towel around his or her own waist and, draping a towel over one arm, moves from person to person in the group pouring water over the bare feet from the pitcher into the bowl. The feet should be rubbed with the hands and dried with the towel.

When the feet have been washed, the basin, ewer and towels should be returned to the table. If Communion is to be celebrated, the leader should wash his or her hands in a separate bowl of water and soap before the consecration of the elements.

The Prayers

These prayers may come from the group. See the prayers for Maundy Thursday in the *Lutheran Service Book Altar Book* or *Lutheran Worship Altar Book*. The group may be encouraged to offer prayers for the strengthening of their own service, prayers for those they serve, and prayers that they might be more receptive to Christ's serving through the service of others. If possible, the Eucharist could be celebrated.

Closing Hymn

"Where Charity and Love Prevail" (*LSB* 845; *HS98* 878)

6 JOURNALING

Journaling can be an important component of a servant event. Providing a quiet time for participants to reflect on their service experience can be a part of each day. These journaling thoughts are adapted from *Engaging Youth in Service-Learning* by Search Institute and could be used to assist participants in their experience.

REFLECTIONS OF A SERVANT JOURNAL

An important element in these studies is to encourage each servant to write a page each day in an ongoing journal that reflects upon his or her attitudes and acts of service and that has been drawn from the study as well as from recent personal experiences. These journals may or may not be shared with other servants or a counselor.

Supplies needed: one copy of journal cover printed on cardstock for each participant, one set of journal pages for each participant, fabric or felt scraps, yarn, construction-paper scraps, sequins, glitter, markers, crayons, scissors, craft glue, glue sticks, hole punch, brass fasteners

Each group member will need a copy of the journal cover.

Instruct the group members that they are to use the supplies provided to make the shape printed on the cover become "a reflection of you."

Assemble the cover and journal pages using the hole punch and brass fasteners or 8-inch pieces of yarn.

Depending on the time when this study is done, reflect either on your hopes for the day or your experiences during the day now completed. The following are suggestions that might get you started. If more time is needed by certain individuals, they may complete this part of the study at another time.

MY STORY OF SERVANTHOOD

Spend personal time writing the first page of your journal. The following are suggestions that might be helpful for getting started.

- Review Luke 10:38–42. Identify in your mind a certain "Martha" in your life and how that person has reflected servanthood in a special way?

- Identify, also, a certain "Mary" in your life and how that person has reflected servanthood in a special way?

- Think of a time, perhaps this day, when you have reflected "Martha" in your own life of servanthood.

- Also, think of a time, perhaps this day, when you have reflected "Mary" in your own life of servanthood.

- Either then, or this day, reflect what Jesus is telling you about His relationship with you and how important that is in your servant role?

- Conclude this chapter of your journal with a short prayer appropriate to what you have studied today.

Servant Studies © 2007 Concordia Publishing House. Okay to copy.

MY STORY OF SERVANTHOOD

Spend personal time writing the **second** page of your journal. The following are suggestions that might be helpful for getting started.

- Review the story of the lost son in Luke 15:11–32.

- Spend a moment reflecting upon your family relationships—how love is shared and servanthood shown.

- Identify in your own mind which of the two brothers you more closely identify with (if possible).

- If you relate to the younger brother, then how have you learned lessons in being loved and showing love?

- If you relate to the older brother, then how have you learned lessons in being loved and showing love?

- Reflect upon the daily challenges and choices parents must make according to God's will.

- Ponder God's unqualified forgiveness toward you and how you reflect that forgiveness to others.

- Spend a moment or two reflecting upon the "must do" jobs you have either as a member of a family or at this Servant Event and how your mindset may change from "obligation" to "willing obedience."

- Conclude this page of your journal with a short prayer appropriate to what you have studied today.

Servant Studies © 2007 Concordia Publishing House. Okay to copy.

MY STORY OF SERVANTHOOD

Spend personal time writing third page of your journal. The following are suggestions that might be helpful for getting started.

 Identify in your own mind another person whom you call "friend" and what qualities make up your friendship.

 Identify in your own mind someone either at home or at the Servant Event who seems to be in need of a friend and how you might serve that person.

 Reflect upon a recent time or circumstance when you befriended another person.

 Reflect upon how important it is in your life to know and believe that Jesus is always and forever your friend.

 Conclude this page of your journal with a short prayer appropriate to what you have studied today.

Servant Studies © 2007 Concordia Publishing House. Okay to copy.

MY STORY OF SERVANTHOOD

Spend personal time writing the fourth page of your journal. The following are suggestions that might be helpful for getting started.

 Spend time reflecting upon a situation when you sincerely confessed your sin and your sin was forgiven in Christ's name and how that experience enabled you to be able to forgive someone else.

 Reflect upon how forgiveness and servanthood are interrelated, perhaps, this very day.

 Reflect upon your privilege to "feed a lamb" (i.e., another person) through a word or act of service recently or, perhaps, this day.

 Reflect upon what Christ's unqualified forgiveness for you daily means to you.

 Conclude this page of your journal with a short prayer appropriate to what you have studied today.

Servant Studies © 2007 Concordia Publishing House. Okay to copy.

MY STORY OF SERVANTHOOD

Spend personal time writing the fifth page of your journal. The following are suggestions that might be helpful for getting started.

 Reflect upon certain gifts God has given you: specifically, if you are a leader, then how you use that gift as a servant, and if you are a follower, then how you use that gift as a servant.

 Identify a specific person who is in authority over you and how that person has reflected servanthood toward you in his or her life.

 Reflect upon how God has guided you through ups and downs to bring you to this time and place in your life.

 Reflect upon how God through His Word and Sacraments has given you a spirit of servanthood.

 Reflect upon the elected leadership of this nation and how you may support them with your prayers.

 Conclude this page of your journal with a short prayer appropriate to what you have studied today.

Servant Studies © 2007 Concordia Publishing House. Okay to copy.

MY STORY OF SERVANTHOOD

Spend personal time writing the sixth and final page of your journal. The following are suggestions that might be helpful for getting started.

 Reflect upon a certain time or circumstance when you ended up doing much more for a particular person than you originally thought your act of service would involve.

 Identify a person in your life who is selfless in showing acts of compassion.

 Reflect upon the lavishness of God's love in your life and how God showers blessings upon you beyond what you deserve or expect.

 Reflect upon a specific person who is in need of agape love and what you might say or do for that person as a loving servant of Christ.

 If possible, think of someone in the immediate community in which you live and how you might be a godly neighbor to that person (or family).

 Conclude this page of your journal with a short prayer appropriate to what you have studied today.

Servant Studies © 2007 Concordia Publishing House. Okay to copy.